THE KEY TO VICTORY

companion volume to *The Impending Drama*

by the author of *Preparation for the Final Crisis*

Fernando Chaij

THE KEY TO VICTORY

companion volume to *The Impending Drama*

by the author of *Preparation for the Final Crisis*

Fernando Chaij

Southern Publishing Association, Nashville, Tennessee

This book was
Edited by Gerald Wheeler
Designed by Mark O'Connor

Type set: 10/11 Palatino

Printed in U.S.A.

Library of Congress Cataloging in Publication Data

Chaij, Fernando.
Key to victory.

1. Christian life—Seventh-day Adventist authors. 2. Holy Spirit. 3. Eschatology. I. Title.
BV4501.2.C45 248'.48'673 79-548
ISBN 0-8127-0224-7

Contents

Key to Abbreviations

AA *The Acts of the Apostles*
BC Ellen G. White's comments in the *Seventh-day Adventist Bible Commentary*
CD *Counsels on Diet and Foods*
CH *Counsels on Health*
ChS *Christian Service*
COL *Christ's Object Lessons*
CT *Counsels to Parents, Teachers, and Students*
CW *Counsels to Writers and Editors*
DA *The Desire of Ages*
Ed *Education*
Ev *Evangelism*
EW *Early Writings*
GC *The Great Controversy*
GW *Gospel Workers*
MH *The Ministry of Healing*
MYP *Messages to Young People*
PK *Prophets and Kings*
PP *Patriarchs and Prophets*
RH *Review and Herald*
SC *Steps to Christ*
1SM *Selected Messages*, Book One (two books)
1T *Testimonies for the Church*, Vol. 1 (nine volumes)
TM *Testimonies to Ministers and Gospel Workers*

Introduction

The subject of this book—our spiritual needs and readiness for the last crisis—interests every Christian. Here we will not concern ourselves with a mere presentation of the important facts and events that in the near future, according to prophecy, will shape the history of the world and shake the very heart of the church. We did that in our previous book, entitled *The Impending Drama,* in which we made a systematic study of last-day events and their meaning to the remnant church.

In accordance with the title of this work, *Key to Victory,* we will study the know-how, the technique, of our preparation, the way to make sure of our readiness for the time of the end.

Since we stand on the threshold of the final crisis, the subjects we approach are of an urgent nature. It is always much easier and more effective to meet a crisis successfully if we have studied the right way of facing it before it actually arrives.

Things are moving rapidly. "We are standing on the threshold of great and solemn events. Many of the prophecies are about to be fulfilled in quick succession. Every element of power is about to be set to work. Past history will be repeated; old controversies will arouse to new life, and peril will beset God's people on every side. Intensity is taking hold of the human family. It is permeating everything upon the earth" (TM 116).

Fanfare will not announce the end of the investigative judgment and the close of probation. Silently, while everyone continues his normal activities, whether good or bad, the last hour will sound in the time clock of God, and the opportunity to make any kind of preparation will vanish forever. As a thief in the night, that hour will come on the world and on the church, and Heaven will issue the decree, "He that is unjust, let him be unjust still" (Revelation 22:11).

But now we still live in the day of grace. Our heavenly High Priest still intercedes on our behalf in the sanctuary above. His Spirit tenderly speaks to human hearts.

It should encourage us that God has made ample provision for our eternal victory, so that we need not enter the time of trouble unprepared. No matter how fierce the battle, no matter how weak we may be because of inherited or cultivated tendencies and habits, the Lord offers to every one of us today the Christian armor, "for the weapons of our warfare are . . . mighty through God to the pulling down of strong holds" (2 Corinthians 10:4).

May God help us to appropriate those tremendously effective weapons and through daily practice to learn how to use them, in order to become a part of the triumphant multitude that will stand on the sea of glass mingled with fire, a multitude composed of those who have achieved the victory.

Chapter 1

The Present Condition of the Church

When we want to get ready for an important appointment, we clean ourselves, comb our hair, and dress properly for the occasion. But we can never be sure of our appearance without using a mirror. The mirror accurately reflects our face, our hair, our dress, our general aspect.

In His Word God has given us a wonderful mirror that depicts the condition of the remnant church and gives us a clear insight into our needs. The message to the church of Laodicea, which applies in general to the Christian people of our days, but particularly to our Seventh-day Adventist Church (3T 252; 4T 87), presents a faithful description of our weaknesses and needs and at the same time points out the only remedy.

The same interest with which we look at ourselves in a mirror prior to meeting an important person should characterize our study and analysis of Revelation 3:14-22. Here, recognizing our spiritual state, begins our real preparation for last-day events.

A Warm Message of Love

The fact that makes this message particularly relevant appears in verses 14 and 15 of the third chapter of Revelation: "These things saith the Amen, the faithful and true witness, the beginning of the creation of God, I know thy works." Many times a witness does not have the moral courage to state the truth because he fears the possible consequences, because he does not want to alienate the defendant, or because he is biased. In this case, though, the

Witness is absolutely impartial, faithful, and true. On the other hand, He thoroughly understands us, declaring, "I know thy works."

Actually it is easy to sincerely deceive ourselves about our own condition. The psalmist prayed, "Search me, O God, and know my heart: try me, and know my thoughts: and see if there be any wicked way in me, and lead me in the way everlasting" (Psalm 139:23, 24). Like Jeremiah (17:9), we must realize that "the heart is deceitful above all things, and desperately wicked." The prophet asked, "Who can know it?"

One of the greatest philosophers of all times said, "Know yourself." Evidently our human tendency to misjudge our own condition intensifies in this Laodicean hour. We desperately need somebody who can tell us the truth, because it is vital to our readiness for the last crisis.

Moreover, the Author of the Laodicean message is One who loves us so much that He voluntarily assumed for Himself human flesh. He went through all the miseries of a human being with his sadnesses, trials, and temptations, and finally offered His life on the cross to save us.

Such a friend will not exaggerate or diminish the truth, neither will He lie. What He tells us in His letter of love springs from His divine and perfect knowledge of our real condition and from His unspeakable love for us. And what does He say about us?

Lukewarmness

"Thou art neither cold nor hot, . . . thou art lukewarm" (Revelation 3:15, 16).

In a Red Cross course on first aid, the instructor explained to us that when a person has swallowed certain poisons, he immediately needs an emetic, or a vomitive. The most handy vomitive is lots of lukewarm water, especially with a little salt added.

Everybody tries to avoid drinking lukewarm water, resorting either to cool or hot water. What does the lukewarmness of Laodicea mean? Indifference, lack of commitment, spiritual neutrality, lack of missionary activity, a superficial experience. Lukewarmness means going through the act of religion without having a real experience with Christ.

Several short statements may open before us a variety of ways in which we can manifest such lukewarmness. "*Professors of religion* are not willing to closely examine themselves to see whether they are in the faith; and it is a fearful fact that many are leaning on a false hope. . . . They seem to think that *a profession of the truth will save them*. . . . It would be more pleasing to the Lord if lukewarm professors of religion had never named His name" (1T 188*).

Commenting on Revelation 3:15, 16, Ellen White says also: "Satan is willing that you should be *Christians in name*, for you can suit his purpose better. If you *have a form and not true godliness*, he can use you to decoy others into the same self-deceived way" (1T 162).

"To those who are *indifferent* at this time Christ's warning is: 'Because thou art lukewarm, and neither cold nor hot, I will spew thee out of my mouth' " (6T 408). "Many of our people are lukewarm. They occupy the position of Meroz, *neither for nor against*, neither cold nor hot. *They hear the words of Christ, but do them not*" (5T 76, 77). And finally: "The great mass of professing Christians will meet with bitter disappointment in the day of God. . . . Lukewarm and *halfhearted*, they dishonor God far more than the avowed unbeliever. They grope in darkness, when they might be walking in the noonday light of the Word" (7BC 970).

On another occasion Mrs. White related the expression "lukewarm" to a lack of evangelistic endeavor. "He who appreciates the love of Christ," she wrote, "will be an earnest worker with Christ to bring other souls as sheaves to the Master. Thorough work is always done by all who are connected with Christ. They bear fruit to His glory. But *indolence* and *carelessness and frivolity* separate the soul from Christ" (TM 130).

"I Will Spew Thee Out of My Mouth"

Fortunately the idea conveyed by the original Greek is

---

*Generally speaking, the emphasis is supplied by the author.

not that with all certainty the Lord *will* spew the church out of His mouth, but that He *is about to*. It is not a prophecy but an admonition, directed not to the whole church, but only to those who do not receive the message and react properly.

No other church arises after Laodicea. She will revive, will arouse from her deadly slumber, and will measure up to the unique challenge she receives from the Lord to finish His work.

It is a pity, though, that a good portion of the church, represented by the parable of the foolish virgins, will not take the message to heart. They force God to cut them from the body of Christ. The rest of the members, the ones that go through the revival and reformation, will receive the outpouring of the Spirit of God in the latter rain and will have the privilege of finishing their task on earth.

Ellen White saw that "some will not bear this straight testimony [called forth by the counsel of the True Witness to the Laodiceans]. They will rise up against it, and this is what will cause a shaking among God's people" (EW 270). Although it is a sad statement, we find consolation in the fact that many of God's children will mend their ways, will look for a real experience with the Lord, and will partake of the victory of God's triumphant church.

The message sounds right now. Now we have the opportunity of changing our lukewarmness. Tomorrow may be late—not only because nobody can foretell the end of probationary time but because none of us has his life assured for one hour.

Long ago the angel had to declare, "Ephraim is joined to idols: let him alone" (Hosea 4:17). Will the Lord have to say that of any of us? "Individuals are tested and proved a length of time to see *if they will sacrifice their idols* and heed the counsel of the True Witness" (1T 187). And among the idols, she mentions selfishness, pride, and evil passions. They produce lukewarmness. We hope that the sealing angel will not need to say of any of us, "So-and-so 'is joined to idols: let him alone.' "

Self-deceit and Spiritual Infatuation

The message to the remnant church contrasts what the

Laodicean claims with what the True Witness declares. To the ones who say, "I am rich, and increased with goods, and have need of nothing," Christ proposes the real condition: "[Thou] knowest not that thou art wretched, and miserable, and poor, and blind, and naked" (Revelation 3:17). Could there be any gloomier description of a human being?

His condition is even worse because he does not know it. An Arabic proverb states, "He that does not know and does not know that he does not know is foolish. Go away from him."

The members of the church afflicted by the Laodicean malady find themselves in a state of self-deception. While full of self-righteousness, at the same time they teach and engage in controversy over the righteousness of Christ, believing that they have it. They forget the best definition we have of "justification by faith": "It is the work of God in laying the glory of man in the dust, and doing for man that which it is not in his power to do for himself. When men see their own nothingness, they are prepared to be clothed with the righteousness of Christ" (TM 456, in part [*Special Testimonies to Ministers and Workers* (Series A, No. 9, 1897), p. 62]).

In *Steps to Christ*, pages 64, 65, Mrs. White wrote that "the closer you come to Jesus, the more faulty you will appear in your own eyes; for your vision will be clearer, and your imperfections will be seen in broad and distinct contrast to His perfect nature. . . . No deep-seated love for Jesus can dwell in the heart that does not realize its own sinfulness. . . . If we do not see our own moral deformity, it is unmistakable evidence that we have not had a view of the beauty and excellence of Christ."

The Laodicean runs a great risk. Naturally he has the conviction that his church is God's true church, that it is the remnant church. The danger lies in the unwitting inference that he may draw: "My church is the church of God. I have the truth. *Hence* I am all right. I am saved."

We must never forget that the mere possession of the right doctrines, of membership in the right church, does not save anybody. It is not knowledge, but experience, we need; not theory, but practice.

The condition of self-deception and spiritual infatuation runs side by side with the lukewarmness described in verses 15 and 16. The word "because" in verse 16 establishes the intimate relationship of both ideas. "Thou art neither cold nor hot . . . *because* thou sayest, I am rich." But thank God there exists a way out, and the True Witness says, "Be zealous therefore, and repent" (verse 19).

Christ Knocking at the Door

Christ goes on to say, "Behold, I stand at the door, and knock: if any man hear my voice, and open the door, I will come in to him, and will sup with him, and he with me" (verse 20).

The artists that draw the wonderful pictures of Christ knocking at the door of the heart traditionally do not paint any knob on the outside. Only the individual himself can open that door from the inside and invite Christ to get in. The Saviour never forces human will. He made man in His own image and provided him with the attributes of responsibility and freedom: free choice, free will. Man's cooperation, his active interest, and his eager willingness, borne of a sense of need, are absolutely indispensable in order for Christ to come into his life and transform him.

Sometimes idols of worldliness and selfishness bar the door of the heart. Self may be so strong that it refuses to let Christ remove it. If the individual does not deny self, if the ego does not die, then Jesus cannot enter to reign on the throne of the heart. He cannot heal us of our spiritual sickness.

Everything can be achieved if Jesus dwells in the heart. But "without me," He said, "ye can do nothing" (John 15:5). Self sometimes manifests itself in an unforgiving spirit, in hate, in hard feelings. When that happens, Christ cannot even forgive our sins because we won't let Him.

With the many differences in temperament that we find among human beings, some may find it difficult to sympathize with one another, and this side of heaven they may never become close friends. But this does not mean that any two persons, no matter how different they are, need to hate each other and maintain an unforgiving spirit.

When we accept Christ into our hearts to let Him teach the daily lessons of meekness we must learn, Jesus gladly enters to be our Lord and permanent Benefactor. Surrendering our will to Him, ready to renounce selfishness, struggle for supremacy, bitterness, or any other sin that cuts us off from Him, we will discover His power to prepare us for the final victory.

If we humbly recognize our own needs, renounce self, and submit to Jesus, He stands ready to change us and to give us peace with God and with everybody else. "To him that overcometh will I grant to sit with me in my throne, even as I also overcame, and am set down with my Father in his throne" (Revelation 3:21).

"He That Hath an Ear"

"He that hath an ear, let him hear what the Spirit saith unto the churches" (verse 22). The emphasis again centers on human decision. The marvelous plan of restoration has existed from the foundation of the world. God has made provision for us. The healing, the victory, can be ours. God longs for it to happen, and it will if we hear, if we take to heart the loving invitation, if we repent and seek God's forgiveness and the deeper experience that will erase our indifference, lukewarmness, self-deception, and self-righteousness.

Chapter 2

The Heart of the Laodicean Message

In spite of progress in medicine during the past few decades and of all the new ways discovered to combat disease there still remain some physical ailments that science cannot heal. The doctor has to limit himself to saying, "We can do nothing to cure the patient. All we can do is give him something to kill the pain." And it is discouraging to see such patients languish in bed and little by little approach the dreaded hour of death without any hope of recovery.

But in the case of the message to Laodicea we deal with the Divine Physician. Having in His able hands all the resources of heaven, He possesses an all-powerful ability to diagnose without error and to heal completely any spiritual malady.

The most important part of the message to Laodicea is its positive aspect, the one that sometimes we give less importance to. After the great Doctor of heaven diagnoses the ailment of the church, He proceeds to write a prescription that will cure His patient's condition. But His prescription can be filled only in the pharmacy of God.

We will study in detail its three great components to see what they are, how to secure them, and how to apply them so that we may get the blessed results. But before doing it, let's address our attention to an enigmatic expression that precedes the prescription itself. Two verses in Revelation 3—18 and 19—contain the whole formula.

"Buy of Me"

Christ says, "Buy of me." In the case of a regular doctor

who urges such a thing after a general checkup and a diagnosis, we would question not only his ethics but also his wisdom and veracity. We would conclude that he was trying to take advantage of his patients, using his profession only to make money, thus degrading his practice.

But here Christ is trying to call to our attention the fact that the spiritual patient should be so willing to secure the medicine prescribed that he is ready to put forth his utmost effort. A passive attitude will never gain him the remedy.

For physical healing, the patient must be open with his doctor, must trust his medical knowledge, must deeply feel his own helplessness, must resolve to put forth all he has within him to cooperate in doing what the doctor prescribes. The sinner must follow a similar course for spiritual healing. Only then will he receive the change from an indifferent, self-deceived, corrupt person into a real child of God—active, full of life, humble, and perfectly sound—with a character prepared for heaven.

The ancient prophet voiced God's offer of mercy when he called, "Ho, every one that thirsteth, come ye to the waters, and he that hath no money; come ye, buy, and eat; yea, come, buy wine and milk without money and without price" (Isaiah 55:1). As we see, Isaiah uses the same verb, "buy," referring to the transaction of securing the water of life, the wine of the Holy Spirit, and the milk of the Word of God. But the buying does not involve money.

We do have a price to pay, though. Paul makes it clear: "Work out your own salvation with fear and trembling" (Philippians 2:12). Each one of us should have an intense desire, an active willingness, that goes to the extent of selling all that he has in order to buy "the pearl of great price" or the hidden treasure of Christ's parable.

Although the prescription does not cost any money, and in that sense is completely free, it does require something much more important. But it is something that anybody has to offer. Everyone can afford it. The price is the full surrender of the heart, the total submission of the will to God. He in turn waits to pour out the most precious treasure of heaven into that life in order to make it pure and happy. When we are willing to be emptied of self, Christ and the

Spirit will fill that vacuum, and our life will never be the same again.

"Gold Tried in the Fire"

The first element Christ offers us in His threefold prescription is gold "tried in the fire." It is 24-karat gold, totally purified. Such gold fills our first spiritual need. Instead of being poor and miserable, we are made immensely rich in spiritual wealth. "I counsel thee to buy of me gold tried in the fire, that thou mayest be rich."

Ellen White tells us that "the gold here recommended . . . is faith and love" (4T 88). If we see in that quotation a figure of synecdoche, we may accept that this wonderful refined gold is the fruit of the Spirit, which is "love, joy, peace, longsuffering, gentleness, goodness, faith, meekness, temperance" (Galatians 5:22, 23). By the way, the word *fruit* is singular, in spite of the fact that the passage mentions several virtues. And it is not a grammatical mistake, because all the characteristics form one unity and are subproducts of love—the fruit by antonomasia—which is the essence of God's nature. Faith, the living bond that connects the human heart with the unlimited resources of heaven, sustains all these qualities.

Only the presence of Christ in our heart may produce real love to God and to man, eradicating all hate and hard feelings and prompting us to service. From the time of his falling into sin, man has been selfish by nature. To change our nature and form a character ready for heaven, we need a miracle of grace that can be wrought only by the presence of Christ. But since Christ does not reside in person in our hearts, He dwells there through the Holy Spirit. And love, along with faith, is the fruit of the Spirit, the natural result of His presence.

The most wonderful definition of love, the one we find in 1 Corinthians 13:4-7, is at the same time the most accurate description of a Christian. So if we substitute our own name instead of "charity" or "love," we have a mirror in which to look at ourselves and know our real needs. All the characteristics that Paul describes we may acquire by uniting ourselves with Christ, combining our weakness with His strength, our ignorance with His wisdom, our impotence with His absolute power. We must surrender ourselves every day to Him, asking for and experiencing the presence of the Spirit continually in our heart.

Faith is the second great aspect of the fruit of the Spirit. It makes real all of God's promises, all His blessings, including love and righteousness. Acting on faith, we allow heaven to come to our life, which makes the presence of God real in our experience.

How do we get the Spirit and all His fruit? Through a live desire manifested in sincere daily supplication and a moment-by-moment surrender to Christ. And since faith is not simply an opinion or a mental acceptance but an active principle, a marvelous transaction in which we accept Christ and submit everything to Him, it produces action and works, it changes our life. Faith, along with prayer, is the key that opens the treasures of heaven.

"White Raiment"

The second element of the heavenly formula is: "I counsel thee to buy of me . . . white raiment, that thou mayest be clothed, and that the shame of thy nakedness do not appear" (verse 18).

When the father in the parable, after a long absence of his son, saw the lad coming back home, the first thing he ordered after embracing him and shedding tears of joy was, "Bring forth the best robe, and put it on him" (Luke 15:22). The boy wore filthy rags. The Laodicean desperately needs a new suit to cover the shame of his nakedness.

Like the garment that the father ordered put on his son, the white raiment that Christ provides to the poor who come to Him is His own righteousness (Revelation 19:8). In the words of Ellen White, "The white raiment is purity of character, the righteousness of Christ imparted to the sinner. This is indeed a garment of heavenly texture, that can be bought only of Christ for a life of willing obedience" (4T 88).

Here the inspired statement speaks of *imparted* righteousness. But we cannot really separate the imparted and the imputed righteousness of Christ. They comprise two different aspects of an integral experience. The imparted righteousness, the character of Christ reproduced in man by the action of the Holy Spirit, needs first imputed righteousness, an experience of recognition of sin, confession, and forgiveness. The imputed righteousness then continues to work simultaneously with the imparted righteousness, giving it efficacy.

The same faith that works justification also brings us to abandon sin, changes our character, and creates obedience in us because it allows the Spirit of God to take possession of the heart and to work effectively in it.

So the white raiment is the righteousness of Christ in its broad aspect. If justification "is our title to heaven," sanctification "is our fitness for heaven" (MYP 35). I may have received as a free gift a ticket to travel to a cold country in midwinter. But unless I have the right clothing, I could not survive in that climate. We need the character of Christ to be able to live in heaven and enjoy it.

"No repentance is genuine that does not work reformation" (DA 555, 556).

Man possesses no merit at all because of imparted righteousness. It is the work of God. The faith which justifies and sanctifies us comes as a free gift from Heaven. Even repentance results from the pleading of the Spirit and of His convicting power.

"Eyesalve"

When a person suffers from glaucoma—an ailment that produces increased pressure within the eyeball—he loses his vision little by little. The ophthalmologist normally prescribes some medicinal eye drops to reduce that pressure and prevent blindness. And the doctor insists that the patient be extremely careful and faithful in using his eye drops several times a day.

Sin produces a loss of spiritual vision. It becomes blurred at first, and if we do nothing, the ailment progresses until at last we no longer perceive any difference between good and evil.

The third important element of the heavenly prescription is: "Anoint thine eyes with eyesalve, that thou mayest see" (verse 18). As we remember, part of the problem was that the Laodicean is blind. "The eyesalve is that wisdom and grace which enables us to discern between the evil and the good, and to detect sin under any guise" (4T 88).

In another place Ellen White states that "the 'eyesalve,' the Word of God, makes the conscience smart under its application; for it convicts of sin. . . . The sinner, beholding himself in God's great moral looking glass, sees himself as God views him, and exercises repentance toward God and faith toward our Lord Jesus Christ" (7BC 965).

Only the Holy Spirit can impart the wisdom and grace that enables us to discern sin. And the Spirit works through the word to bring conviction. In other words, the combination of the study of God's Word, as well as of the writings of Ellen G. White, and our daily request for the Holy Spirit in our life provides us with spiritual eye drops, restores our full vision, and completes our healing process. The more we study the Word, the more we ask and receive the Spirit, the more we will become aware of deficiencies and defects of character, the more we will be spiritually sensitive, and the more we will benefit from the experience of repentance.

"I Rebuke and Chasten"

Christ thoughtfully explains what He must do so we will not get discouraged when it happens: "As many as I love, I rebuke and chasten" (verse 19). As an understanding doctor who had to take the same medicine Himself, He puts forth extra effort to encourage us. When He was a human being like any one of us here on earth, in spite of the fact that He was absolutely sinless, He profited from pain. "Though he were a Son, yet learned he obedience by the things which he suffered; and being made perfect, he became the author of eternal salvation unto all them that obey him" (Hebrews 5:8).

If the discipline of trials and chastisement was good for the Son of God while He was a man, how much more it will be a blessing for us, and how much more we need such an experience to prepare our characters to meet the Lord. "Now," Paul said, "no chastening for the present seemeth to be joyous, but grievous: nevertheless afterward it yieldeth the peaceable fruit of righteousness unto them which are exercised thereby. Wherefore lift up the hands which hang down, and the feeble knees" (Hebrews 12:11, 12).

The apparently harsh words spoken by the True Witness, the dim view about our condition, the discouraging description of the church, come only for the purpose of turning us back from our self-deception and our false confidence and directing us to the true source of purity and justice.

God at times allows the enemy to afflict us in order to make us more sensitive to the voice of His Spirit, more aware of our needs, and more willing to seek His triple remedy that can heal us completely.

Sometimes He needs to allow us to suffer in order to lead us to a state where our hearts may be in tune with Heaven. Only then will we be able to receive the message He wants to send us. But we may be sure that when we pass through "the water of affliction" the Lord is nearer to us than ever before, and His love sustains us. And afterwards we will realize how the Lord has taken care of us and will feel gratitude for the manifestation of His love.

Every one of us needs a specific kind of help. Our heavenly Father sends the chastisement that in His providence will give us precisely that aid. And when we reach heaven our guardian angel will explain to us all the mysteries of our life, all the whys that here do not have an answer, all the reasons for our perplexities.

"Be Zealous Therefore, and Repent"

These words, some of the last of the True Witness, should encourage us. They show that we have not reached the point of no return. He hopes that many will heed His counsel.

Some may consider repentance more or less an isolated act that happens to spiritual beginners. But nothing is farther from the truth. Repentance is a permanent experience that accompanies us through our whole life, making us more responsive to God's voice. After all, repentance—that is, sorrow for sin and a turning away from it—is the proper response of our heart to the voice of the Spirit.

And the farther we travel the Christian road, the more we experience real repentance. It continually takes us back to God to seek forgiveness and victory, imputed and imparted righteousness, justification and sanctification, cleansing from sin, and purity of heart.

Perfection does not come easy. It takes strenuous effort, perseverance, hard battles, especially with self. At times it involves defeat, tears, and confession. Always it demands new and more complete surrender to God. We inherit weaknesses from our ancestors, and we develop and acquire other bad tendencies. But the patience of God continues to surround us, keeps on giving us new opportunities to learn the lessons we need in our individual life. For some the road may seem longer and harder than for others, but everyone can receive strength enough to endure the struggles, and through them he can acquire the qualities of character needed to finally receive the seal of the living God.

Chapter 3

The Shaking

One of the most outstanding signs that we are approaching the end of time is the fierceness with which the enemy attacks the church as a whole—both from the outside and from the inside—and every true follower of Christ individually. We live in the time of the "shaking."

In ancient times—and even today they still do it in primitive areas of the world—farmers would shake the wheat in a sieve so that the broken kernels, husks, and foreign particles might fall through the mesh and the chaff be blown away. Scripture uses the illustration several times to refer to the refining and selecting of His people, a process that will have to take place in preparation for a time of crisis. Now, in the last days, He will have to make a final separation between the wheat and the tares through the "shaking" or the "sifting," two equivalent terms used in the Bible and in the writings of Ellen G. White to indicate this divinely directed action.

But the shaking is not only a collective work that affects the church as a whole. It is also an individual process that begins the day the person accepts Christ and ends the day his probation closes, whether because of his death or because the investigative judgment has ended. To Peter, in a critical hour of his life, the Lord said, "Simon, Simon, behold, Satan hath desired to have you, that he may sift you as wheat: but I have prayed for thee, that thy faith fail not" (Luke 22:31, 32). Incidentally, notice that God does not send the trials and tribulations that constitute the sieve in which we are shaken or sifted. It is Satan. God gives him permission to go only so far, as in the case of Job.

And what God does with every one of us individually to prepare us for heaven, He has done many times with His people as a whole. In Amos 9:9 we read: "I will sift the house of Israel among all nations, like as corn is sifted in a sieve, yet shall not the least grain fall upon the earth." Amos here refers to a dispersion of His people among the heathen nations. God would allow them to suffer affliction and pain so that they would realize their deteriorated spiritual condition and turn back to Him in search of help and change.

Why is it necessary for the shaking experience, then, to take place in God's church? What God has done over and over throughout history to purify His church, He is doing right now more thoroughly because of the special role that the remnant has to play, because of the special level of godliness it has to achieve, and because of the special crisis through which it will pass.

History moves ahead rapidly. Through the power of God, His children will preach the eternal gospel to every person in the world. For this to happen, God will have to pour the mighty showers of the latter rain on the church. But Mrs. White specifies that it cannot occur until the majority of God's people are really converted, until they have accepted in their life the message of the True Witness and have passed through the revival and reformation—and also are actively engaged in witnessing. So the shaking process precedes and prepares for this sequence of events and continues to be simultaneous with it until the end of probation.

Description and Essence

Winds of persecution, of false doctrines, of internal bitterness and disruption or simply an unwillingness to obey the voice of the Spirit and to detach themselves from selfishness and worldliness will blow many away from the church. They need to renounce their idols and by a full surrender to the Lord conquer their sins and weaknesses.

When God allows us to go through the sifting, His only desire is to purify us, to help empty us of self in order for

Him to fill us with His Spirit. As in the case of Peter, He assures us that He has prayed for us that our faith will not fail. He expects us to become whole, since He tells us, as He told Peter, "When thou art converted, strengthen thy brethren" (Luke 22:32).

God waits for His people to come back to Him. "God is sifting His people," Mrs. White wrote. "He *will have* a clean and holy church. We cannot read the heart of man. But the Lord has provided means to keep the church pure" (1T 99).

Causes That Produce the Shaking

Four main causes bring about the shaking. These we will review in succession.

1. *Indifference and carelessness.*

In the chapter of *Early Writings* entitled "The Shaking," Mrs. White relates a vision she had on the subject. In it she impressively describes the struggle through which the people of God were going. Evil angels pressed around the company of wrestling Christians and tried to surround them with increasing darkness. But she saw them "with strong faith and agonizing cries, pleading with God" (EW 269). The only way they could be safe in this "poisonous atmosphere of evil angels" was to keep looking upward to Jesus.

Meanwhile she saw some that seemed *indifferent* and *careless*. They did not follow the example of the other ones "struggling with all their power to resist the evil angels and trying to help themselves by calling upon God with perseverance" (p. 270).

Her vision shows that the general causes why some were shaken out were indifference, carelessness, lack of agonizing prayer and watchfulness in a perilous time.

2. *Lack of firmness in the time of Sunday legislation.*

Describing what we have ahead of us in the enforcement of the Sunday law and the hardships that we will find, Mrs. White wrote, "The time is not far distant when the test will come to every soul. The mark of the beast will be urged upon us. Those who have step by step yielded to worldly demands and conformed to worldly customs will not find it a hard matter to yield to the powers that be, rather than subject themselves to derision, insult, threatened imprisonment, and death. . . . In this time the gold will be separated from the dross in the church" (5T 81). "Many will be called to speak before councils and in courts of justice, perhaps separately and alone" (5T 463).

3. *False doctrines and theological controversies.*

Speaking about a third cause of the sifting process, Ellen White stated that, "there is to be a shaking among God's people; but this is not the present truth to carry to the churches. It will be the result of refusing the truth presented.

"The ministers should not feel that they have some wonderful advanced ideas, and unless all receive these, they will be shaken out, and a people will arise to go forward and upward to the victory. Satan's object is accomplished just as surely when men run ahead of Christ and do the work He has never entrusted to their hands, as when they remain in the Laodicean state" (2SM 13).

Elsewhere she said, "When the shaking comes, *by the introduction of false theories,* these surface readers, anchored nowhere, are like shifting sand" (TM 112).

No one knows exactly which shape the shaking will take in sifting him, for Satan adapts his trials to every individual life. It may assume the guise of some pseudoreform movement that wants to "purify" the leadership or even the traditional theology of the church. Or it may even come as a highly theological and scholarly discussion of a basic truth.

What Satan wants is to divert our attention from our spiritual and individual needs, even forcing us to take sides in a semantic problem that may not have any importance. He wants us, for example, to lose sight of the vital fact that righteousness by faith is not a theory or a doctrine but an experience. Satan wants to involve us in a big argument that will divide the church, if possible, so that some would lose confidence in the great fundamental concepts that we as a church have received and cherished through much study and prayer, truths that have been confirmed by the Word of God and the powerful testimony of the spirit of prophecy.

Only a living, daily experience with Christ, an experiential knowledge of God, will protect us from falling out under the impact of the shaking.

4. *Rejection of the True Witness.*

Mrs. White clearly presented the main cause of the shaking when she wrote, "I asked the meaning of the shaking I had seen and was shown that it would be caused by the *straight testimony called forth by the counsel of the True Witness* to the Laodiceans. This will have its effect upon the heart of the receiver, and will lead him to exalt the standard and pour forth the straight truth. *Some will not bear this straight testimony.* They will rise up against it, and this is what will cause a shaking among God's people" (EW 270).

It is important that we fully understand her statement. Evidently the presentation of the message to Laodicea will divide the church and reveal who are fully committed to Christ and who have only a form of religion without a personal relationship with Him.

The first group, accepting the counsel of the True Witness, will develop the attributes of involvement, steadfastness, and a real desire to achieve sanctification. They will exalt the standard of Christ.

What does the True Witness seek to teach us? "There must be a revival of the strait testimony. The path to heaven is no smoother now than in the days of our Saviour. All our sins must be put away. Every darling indulgence that hinders our religious life must be cut off. The right eye or the right hand must be sacrificed if it cause us to offend. Are we willing to renounce our own wisdom and to receive the kingdom of heaven as a little child? Are we willing to part with self-righteousness? Are we willing to give up our chosen worldly associates? Are we willing to sacrifice the approbation of men?" (5T 222).

"If the professed people of God find their heart opposed to this straight work, it should convince them that they have a work to do to overcome, if they would not be spewed out of the mouth of the Lord. . . . Some are willing to receive one point; but when God brings them to another testing point, they shrink from it and stand back, because they find that it strikes directly at some cherished idol. . . . Those who come up to every point, and stand every test, and overcome, be the price what it may, have heeded the counsel of the True Witness, and they will receive the latter rain, and thus be fitted for translation" (1T 187).

Passing through revival and reformation, those who respond to the True Witness will be different. Their behavior, their homes, their families, will demonstrate the truth they teach. They will be fervent men and women of prayer. No worldliness or selfishness will taint their character. At the same time they will not be silent but will proclaim God's truth.

The message to Laodicea will not affect the other kind of members. Indifferent and careless, they refuse to let the counsel mold and shape their lives. The lives and the words of those transformed by the impact of the True Witness will bother them. Unable to bear the testimony lived and spoken by both consecrated preachers and laymen, they "will rise up against the truth." They will consider the work of the Holy Spirit as fanaticism and extremism. Shaken out, they will abandon God's people, and in many cases they will align themselves with the enemy.

The Time

We do not need to devote much space to the fact that we already live in the time of the shaking. Actually it began immediately after the 1844 disappointment and has continued since then. Nevertheless, the enemy will redouble his efforts, and we may see many defections. Sometimes we may see even gifted leaders drifting away.

Ellen White, in her vision on the shaking, saw that after a while the group of Christians struggling against the darkness pressed upon them by the evil angels decreased in number. Some, under the pressure, had been sifted out.

Over and over Ellen White warns us that the shaking is now in process, and it will continue with renewed strength until the end of probation. To this time apply especially the words of Revelation 12:12: "The devil is come down unto you, having great wrath, because he knoweth that he hath but a short time." Many times he is more aware of the time we live in than we are.

But the encouraging thought is that many will accept the

counsel of the True Witness and will receive its full benefit. They will be ready for Jesus to come. May every one of us be counted among them.

The Church Will Not Fall

Another bright reality should encourage us: The church will not collapse. "The church may appear as about to fall, but it does not fall. It remains, while the sinners in Zion will be sifted out—the chaff separated from the precious wheat" (2SM 380).

In her vision the servant of God saw that the struggling, pleading multitude remained faithful until their final success. "I heard those clothed with the armor speak forth the truth with great power. It had effect" (EW 271).

Actually nothing can detach us from the love of God and from the heavenly source of power—not even life's greatest calamities—if through God's grace we have no sin in our life. When Paul asked, "Who shall separate us from the love of Christ?" he enumerated the worst things that can happen to a human being: "tribulation, or distress, or persecution, or famine, or nakedness, or peril, or sword?" Then he answered, "In all these things we are more than conquerors through him that loved us." And he emphasized even more his thought by declaring, "I am persuaded that neither death, nor life, nor angels, nor principalities, nor powers, nor things present, nor things to come, nor height, nor depth, nor any other creature, shall be able to separate us from the love of God, which is in Christ Jesus our Lord" (Romans 8: 35, 37, 38).

Thank God for such certainty. And thank Him also for the surety that the Seventh-day Adventist Church is the one that will evangelize the earth and will meet the Lord.

How to Avoid Falling

And now we arrive at the last question, a practical one of eternal consequences: How can we avoid being shaken out?

We never should allow a false confidence to take hold of us. When Peter assured Jesus that he would follow Him to the end, even if all the rest deserted Him, he walked on dangerous ground, and Jesus foretold that he would reject Him three times that night.

But when as a consequence of that sad experience he was fully converted and had lost his self-confidence, he put himself where God could transform him. Not too many days after his shameful denial he stood before the Sanhedrin and, with great confidence, even defying death, told the authorities that he would be obedient to God rather than to men.

The victory does not belong to a people naturally valiant. No personal condition or quality will guarantee us the triumph but only a living daily relationship with Christ, which manifests itself in an absolute dependence on Him and the complete submission of total commitment. Paul admonishes us, "Let him that thinketh he standeth take heed lest he fall" (1 Corinthians 10:12). "Without me ye can do nothing," said Christ in John 15:5. Our only source of certainty is Jesus.

Now, how do we relate ourselves with Christ in order not to fall? How do we allow Him to do His miraculous work in our life?

In the vision of the shaking (EW 269-273) Ellen White explains that she saw two classes of Christians: the first class consisted of the indifferent and careless—the ones that did not have a life of prayer and of Bible study. They made no effort to resist the darkness around them. Finally shaken out, they left God's people.

The other class of Christians gives us the key to success. Mrs. White saw them at first pleading and agonizing. Later she refers again to them in the following words: "I was shown those whom I had before seen weeping and praying in agony of spirit. The company of guardian angels around them had been doubled, and they were clothed with an armor from their head to their feet. They . . . obtained the victory" (p. 271).

The times in which we live demand a dedication and seriousness that make us agonize in prayer and search for spiritual truth with a new interest. A shallow experience will prove insufficient during the shaking. A lack of full commitment will be deadly in this time of crisis.

Drawn to our knees, we will learn how to pray as never before as we search for a closer experience with God. And we will study and meditate on the Word with new interest.

But it will also cause us to work for Christ. "We are in the shaking time," wrote Ellen White, "the time when everything that can be shaken will be shaken. The Lord will not excuse those who know the truth if they do not in word and deed obey His command. If we make no efforts to win souls to Christ we shall be held responsible for the work we might have done, but did not do because of our spiritual indolence. Those who belong to the Lord's kingdom must work earnestly for the saving of souls. They must do their part to bind up the law and seal it among the disciples" (6T 332).

While the shaking cleanses the church, while many desert the ranks of the church militant, what will happen with me? Will I be with the indifferent, with the unconcerned? Or will I belong to the group that pray and struggle for a closer relationship with God, and so remain with the winners? This is God's plan for everyone. He has made provision for our success. Our attitude will determine the results.

Chapter 4

Revival and Reformation

Ellen White writes in *Christ's Object Lessons*, page 415, that "the last message of mercy to be given to the world is *a revelation of His character of love.*" Another brief sentence reinforces the previous one: "The children of God are to manifest His glory. *In their own life and character they are to reveal what the grace of God* has done for them" (*ibid.*, 415, 416).

If the essence of the final message of mercy that the world needs is a manifestation of Christ's love in the life of the messengers, we can understand why the following inspired words have become so relevant and so often quoted: "A revival of true godliness among us is the greatest and most urgent of all our needs. To seek this should be our first work" (1SM 121).

Need of a Revival and Reformation

Mrs. White gives another great reason why this work is so vital: "God's people will not endure the test unless there is a revival and a reformation" (7T 285). We require a revival to arouse ourselves to our spiritual needs and recapture our full vitality. Also we need reformation, a reorganization of our life, to make permanent that new spark of spiritual vigor and consecration. Our individual lives, our homes, our churches, and our institutions and offices need a reformation.

Selfishness still lurks in our hearts and in our relations with others. Pride, worldliness, strife for supremacy, selfish ambitions, and impurity still taint us. Many of us, in our lukewarm condition, have lost our first love and lowered our standards. Our children and young people do not receive in many cases, the example of loyalty, consecration, and love that would allow them to withstand temptation.

As a people we still hold the same old standards, but unfortunately in some of our local churches, institutions, homes, and in many of our lives we have consistently lowered such norms. As a consequence, it is difficult for non-Adventists to see much difference between us and the world. We confuse our own young people with our laxity and our lack of adherence to the high principles that have made the Seventh-day Adventist Church a different people.

Certainly we need a revival and a reformation before the Lord can fulfill His promise of the latter rain and before He can work the tremendous miracles we will witness on the eve of His glorious coming. As a people we must have a revival to attract the multitudes and finish the gospel. Reformation must come before the sealing can be finished and we can endure through the time of trouble.

Discovering Satanic Counterfeits

Mrs. White has assured us that Seventh-day Adventists will soon witness spiritual renewal: "Before the final visitation of God's judgments upon the earth there will be among the people of the Lord such a revival of primitive godliness as has not been witnessed since apostolic times" (GC 464).

But Satan has made plans to counteract it. He will try to accomplish this by using several methods, but especially by introducing a counterfeit in order to confuse and seduce, if possible, God's people themselves and at the same time to annul or make void the true reformation.

"The enemy of souls desires to hinder this work [the revival of primitive godliness]; and before the time for such a movement shall come, he will endeavor to prevent it by introducing a counterfeit. In those churches which he can bring under his deceptive power he will make it appear that God's special blessing is poured out; there will be manifest what is thought to be great religious interest. Multitudes will exult that God is working marvelously for them, when the work is that of another spirit. Under a religious guise, Satan will seek to extend his influence over the Christian world" (*ibid.*).

In our own day we have seen many so-called revivals excite the emotions and create a climate of great agitation, but they were totally superficial and did not result in any real reform in the life of the people involved. Without trying to be too judgmental, we have observed this occurring in the "Jesus movements" and in the "charismatic renewals."

The fact remains, though, that there will arise a true "revival of primitive godliness" among the people of God, and we should be happy and grateful for this assurance. Also, we should prepare ourselves to be part of it.

Besides a counterfeit, Satan will employ other favorite means to nullify the true reformation. He will create a spirit of strife and disagreement, which runs side by side with a destructive criticism of the leadership on the one hand and fanaticism on the other.

Whenever we see a spirit of antagonism toward the church we may be absolutely sure that it is not the work of God but of the enemy, no matter if its proponents do it under the guise of a reform to cleanse the church. Mrs. White said that the first thing to disappear when the true revival and reformation begins is the attitude of revolt and destructiveness. "When this reformation begins, the spirit of prayer will actuate every believer and *will banish from the church the spirit of discord and strife*" (8T 251).

Balance and moderation will characterize every true reform movement. The church does not need emotionalism or extremism but a real change of life. Christianity witnessed no strife at Pentecost when the most dramatic revival and reformation of all times occurred. No destructive attacks against anybody, but a spirit of unity, piety, meekness, and prayer as never before. They are the genuine marks of true reformation.

New Light

Often pseudoreformers raise the flag of "new light." There is nothing wrong about new insights and understandings. Actually we should always be looking for new revelations of the great truths of the Bible, new discoveries, and new views to widen our understanding of God's message. "The rebuke of the Lord will rest upon those who would bar the way, that clearer light shall not come to the people" (GW 304).

"Some have asked me if I thought there was any more light for the people of God. Our minds have become so narrow that we do not seem to understand that the Lord has a mighty work to do for us. *Increasing light is to shine upon us;* for 'the path of the just is as the shining light, that shineth more and more unto the perfect day' " (CW 34, 35).

Wider panoramas and new vistas will enrich our understanding of the wonderful system of truth we have as God's people. Probably some up-to-now-unfulfilled prophecies about future events will open to our minds. Richer insights of the basic truths of salvation will bless us as a deeper study goes on, aided by the Holy Spirit.

But any so-called new light must meet at least two indispensable conditions. The first is that the new light will not contradict what God has already given us as a people. "To the law and to the testimony: if they speak not according to this word, it is because there is no light in them" (Isaiah 8:20). Any new light must agree with the former. The Lord is not a God of contradictions, but of harmony (5T 291-295).

The second requisite is that the ones who claim to have found new light must demonstrate no sense of pride, no feeling of superiority, and they must have a willingness to let others analyze and test their concepts and understanding. Anyone claiming to be the only instrument of God to convey a message to the church, while God, in his opinion, bypassed all the rest, disqualifies himself and his message (5T 291).

So we must carefully evaluate any claim of new light within the framework of the preceding safeguards. Ample room exists for a variety of views in many aspects of the great doctrines of the Bible, because every individual may see some facets of the same truth more distinctly than others. Nevertheless, the great pillars of our church, arrived at by our people after great effort, deep study, the leading of the Spirit, and the confirmation of Ellen White, are unmovable.

Signs of True Reformation

Any true reformation begins with results seen in the life of the reformers and the reformed. When Jesus spoke of false prophets He added, "Ye shall know them by their fruits" (Matthew 7:15, 16). No possible reformation can take place without a corresponding concern for one's own condition. It engenders a spirit of fervent supplication on behalf of himself and of intercession on behalf of others.

In a special vision Ellen White saw "a great reformatory movement" in the midst of the church. Praise, intercession, and a genuine conversion aroused by the Holy Spirit accompanied it. As a result, not only did she observe a change in people's lives, but they started a unique witnessing program, and doors opened everywhere for the proclamation of the gospel (9T 126). The core of a revival is the human heart. No change can occur in the church if it does not first begin in the individual.

Reformation and Specifics

Years ago I attended a Wednesday evening meeting. The subject that night was revival and reformation. Unfortunately, in dealing with the vital issue, the minister made a few jokes and ridiculed the matter by referring to the length of the skirts and other similar external issues. His attitude diluted and dismissed the whole subject. Disappointed, I consoled myself with the fact that he was an exception among ministers. But he may typify what some members of the church think.

The kind of reformation we need as individuals and as a people is a true repentance and a complete conversion—a total union with Christ renewed every day and a permanent indwelling of His Spirit in our heart.

But a real change of heart also will take care of all aspects of life and will produce perfect conformity with the will of God. Changing our thinking, our talking, our feelings, our behavior, it will bring every thought into obedience to

God. But also it will manifest itself in our dressing, in our eating, in our social relationship, in the music we listen to, in our reading, in the programs we attend, in our use of radio and television.

Reformation will transform the life in our homes, our churches, and our institutions. The principles that we stand for as a people we will once more uphold and fulfill.

How to Achieve Revival and Reformation

Revival begins at the heart—the mind, the emotions, the will—and results from the indwelling of Christ in us. "If any man be in Christ, he is a new creature: old things are passed away; behold, all things are become new" (2 Corinthians 5:17). A real reformation embraces everything. The apostle Paul conveyed in different words the same great idea that Christ in the heart transforms our whole life; "Be not conformed to this world: but be ye transformed by the renewing of your mind, that ye may prove what is that good, and acceptable, and perfect, will of God" (Romans 12:2).

Trying to achieve reformation merely by correcting some externals may become useless legalism. Real conversion begins at the source of life, at the heart. The opposite would be to try to heal a grave physical ailment just by suppressing pain, combating the symptoms, and leaving active the pathological agent.

While it is good to pay attention to the symptoms, we must find out what the real cause of trouble is. Mrs. White tells us that "circumstances cannot work reforms. Christianity proposes a reformation in the heart. What Christ works within, will be worked out under the dictation of a converted intellect. *The plan of beginning outside and trying to work inward has always failed, and always will fail.* God's plan with you is to begin at the very seat of all difficulties, the heart, and then from out of the heart will issue the principles of righteousness" (CD 35).

But we have also assurance that "the reformation will be *outward as well as inward*" (*ibid.*).

Only the Holy Spirit can change the heart. He is always ready to work on behalf of every person. The only reason why many times He does not work is because the human agent will not permit Him to do so. The human part, insignificant though it may appear to be, is indispensable.

How does man allow the Spirit of God to work?

Here are the simple steps:

1. Give the Spirit a chance to talk to you and impress your mind with your spiritual needs.

There exists only one way of offering the Spirit this opportunity—exposing our mind to Him in the quiet hour of private study of the word—in the Bible and in the writings of Ellen G. White—and in the calm moments of private prayer.

This requires time. We need to include in our daily schedule, preferably in the morning before taking up our regular duties, time enough to be alone with God, reading, meditating, and speaking with Him. Is it too much to devote from half an hour to one hour to this vital devotion?

"Through the living and eternal word of God you have been born again" (1 Peter 1:23, TEV*). The Word is the sword of the Spirit. If we read and meditate upon it for no other purpose than to hear the voice of the Spirit, He will speak to our heart.

The Word of God contains spiritual life. The study or the hearing of the Word sparked all revivals and reformations in the past: in ancient Israel—for example in the time of Josiah—in the Protestant Reformation days, in the time of the Advent movement, and in the few years subsequent to 1888. We should open our minds to the work of the Spirit as faithfully as we eat material food. If we become careless about our daily spiritual food and our private prayer, we begin to lose strength and vitality, and if we persist, we die. On the other hand we increase the vigor of our Christian life to the extent we practice Bible study and private prayer.

Jesus said, "Except ye eat the flesh of the Son of man, and drink his blood, ye have no life in you" (John 6:53). We must feed on the Bible.

2. Try to obey the prompting of the Spirit. "Quench not

---

*From The Bible in Today's English Version. Copyright, American Bible Society, 1976.

the Spirit" (1 Thessalonians 5:19). "Grieve not the holy Spirit of God" (Ephesians 4:30).

If He shows you a defect or weakness of character and puts in you a desire to overcome it, claim His help. With fervent prayer request forgiveness and the presence of Christ, and you will experience victory. When He points out hate or bitterness in your heart and prompts you to change your sentiments, pray about it and act with faith, and in the name of Jesus forgive and put love in your heart. As the Lord convinces you of selfishness, worldliness, and indolence agonize in prayer until God leads you in triumph over them.

Obey the Spirit.

By practicing this double habit we will be on our way toward a wonderful experience that will bring the revival and the reformation we need to meet the Lord.

Chapter 5

Righteousness by Faith

One of the greatest truths of the Bible—righteousness by faith—pervades Scripture from Genesis to Revelation. It is so basic and so vital that Satan puts forth his greatest efforts to prevent real understanding of it. "The enemy of man and God," Mrs. White said, "is not willing that this truth [justification by faith] should be clearly presented; for he knows that if the people receive it fully, his power will be broken" (RH, September 3, 1889).

What our adversary especially wants is to prevent it from becoming an experience in the life of God's children, for it is clear that if they do not achieve it, they lack the real foundation they need in their spiritual life.

Whether certain specific expressions used by the apostle Paul refer only to justification or also to sanctification is immaterial and should be decided by each one. The important thing is that the sanctification is vibrant and alive in all the writings of Paul and all through the Bible, and that righteousness by faith, in order to be real and complete, needs to embrace justification as well as sanctification (MYP 35), forgiveness as well as obedience, pardoning of sin as well as deliverance from it, and that the same faith and the same power that works the first miracle—forgiveness—also produces the second one—transformation of character.

Thus it would please Satan if he could divide the church by theological discussions on it, stir up controversy that would overemphasize one particular aspect while shadowing or hiding another one, so as to give a partial and distorted picture of what the Word of God presents. He would take to a theoretical and apologetic level something that we can understand and benefit from only if the knowledge becomes experiential.

We should consider ourselves fortunate as a people for possessing a great amount of valuable material published on the topic. Ellen White has developed the subject with such simplicity and clarity that no sincere student needs to miss the point or to be deceived by any partial view. Many other books present it thoroughly. Also the *Adventist Review* puts out a wealth of excellent and well-balanced articles.

Need of Righteousness

It is unnecessary to devote much space to deal with the universal need of righteousness. Paul says, "By one man sin entered into the world, and death by sin; . . . for that all have sinned" (Romans 5:12). After the fall of our first parents, the human race and human nature became sinful. David wrote, "I was shapen in iniquity; and in sin did my mother conceive me" (Psalm 51:5).

Man not only lost his sinless condition, but his nature deteriorated in such a way that human flesh now brings with it the germ of sin. This principle, or law, of sin, implanted in the human heart, manifests itself naturally and develops as the years go by. Unless God works a transformation, selfishness, impurity, envy, hatred, covetousness, and other bad traits dominate the life.

There exists just one remedy for sin and sinfulness: the blood of Jesus and the abiding presence of the Master in man's heart. When He gave the wonderful invitation in Matthew 11:28, "Come unto me, all ye that labour and are heavy laden, and I will give you rest," He was speaking especially about the heavy burden of sin that robs man of his happiness and deprives him of spiritual rest. Actually sin is the main problem of every son of Adam, not only because of the eternal consequence but also because it oppresses the conscience, afflicting man with a sense of guilt and unhappiness.

No treatment, no psychology, no psychiatry, no

therapeutic human method, will remove the guilt complex. We find just one great healing and effective remedy: Christ.

Man's Method Versus God's

There can be no peace and rest without justification. When someone is unjust and a sinner subject to death, "justification" is to make him right, or just, and worthy of salvation.

Human history shows that man has a tendency to look for that justification or righteousness in himself, in human methods, or in human sources. But in spite of all his efforts, he continues with the same anguish, the same guilt, the same anxiety, the same spiritual disease, that has characterized his life through all history.

The apostle described the only two methods of searching for righteousness when he wrote, "Not having mine own righteousness, which is of the law, but that which is through the faith of Christ, the righteousness which is of God by faith" (Philippians 3:9).

Here Paul presents man's method: "mine own righteousness." From the days of the first murderer, humanity has tried the wrong way, the impossible road. Nobody can find a way out from the great problem of sin by himself. Cain was too proud to accept God's method, and he dispensed with the lamb that would have proved his faith in and recognition of the Lamb of God, and would have demonstrated his obedience. He resorted to something that God could not accept because it was devoid of any meaning except self-righteousness.

Even before Cain, Adam himself, then polluted by sin, made for himself an apron from the leaves of a fig tree. But it was useless. God had to take the skin of a slain animal, which typified the True Sacrifice, and provide an effective covering robe for him.

The only effective method of justification is God's: the "righteousness of God . . . by faith" (Romans 3:21) in Jesus Christ. "By the deeds of the law there shall no flesh be justified in his sight" (verse 20). Since "all have sinned, and come short of the glory of God" (verse 23), no amount of human effort or good works can atone for past sins, even if from now on we could be perfect. The truth is, though, that "all our righteousnesses are as filthy rags" (Isaiah 64:6). Even our best works, apart from God, are contaminated with selfishness and tainted with sin, and in the sight of our heavenly Father they are filthy rags.

Only the righteousness of God, received by faith in Jesus, can save man. God and Jesus paid the price. We must humbly accept it by faith, recognizing our spiritual nakedness and the total futility of our human efforts. Apart from God, man has no power to be righteous. Only "the Lord [is] our righteousness" (Jeremiah 23:6).

Imputed and Imparted Righteousness

The reason why we have seen so much discussion regarding the relative importance of the two terms is because some separate the two. They seem to imply that we find two kinds of righteousness of Christ, and then they begin to argue about which one is the more vital or important, or which one saves us.

But in reality we cannot divide them. There is just one righteousness, the righteousness of Christ, received by faith. The imputed and the imparted righteousness represent two different stages, or aspects, of the same great experience centered in Christ. Imputed righteousness, in a sense, comes first, because it implies repentance and confession of sin, and the immediate result is forgiveness, or justification. But we continue to need it all our life because of our sinful nature. In spite of all our spiritual development and progress, until the end of the time of grace we will continually have to avail ourselves of the merits of the perfect life and the vicarious death of Christ both for justification and sanctification.

Imputed righteousness we achieve when through faith we ask God to credit or transfer to us the merits of our Lord Jesus. It is a perfect and sufficient righteousness, no matter how big our debt, no matter how great our need or how terrible our sins or mistakes. The wonderful robe of His righteousness covers us completely so that when God looks at us from heaven He does not see us, but He sees His perfect and beloved Son. Scriptures such as Romans 3:24,

25, 28; Ephesians 2:8; Romans 3:20; 1 John 1:7-9; Romans 5:1; and many more sustantiate this wonderful reality.

In an enlightening paragraph, Ellen White explains imputed righteousness in this way: "The only way in which he [the sinner] can attain to righteousness is through faith. By faith he can bring to God the merits of Christ, and the Lord places the obedience of His Son to the sinner's account. Christ's righteousness is accepted in place of man's failure, and God receives, pardons, justifies, the repentant, believing soul, treats him as though he were righteous, and loves him as He loves His Son. This is how faith is accounted righteousness; and the pardoned soul goes on from grace to grace, from light to a greater light" (1SM 367).

But at the same time true justification leads the child of God to the next immediate stage, to the imparted righteousness. "The righteousness of Christ is not a cloak to cover unconfessed and unforsaken sin; it is a principle of life that transforms the character and controls the conduct. Holiness is wholeness for God; it is the entire surrender of heart and life to the indwelling of the principles of heaven" (DA 555, 556).

The Christian achieves justification by faith. But faith has immediate results, or otherwise it is not a true saving faith. "Faith, if it hath not works, is dead. . . . shew me thy faith without thy works, and I will shew thee my faith by my works" (James 2:17, 18). The apostle emphasizes his thought again with an apparently strange statement: "Ye see then how that by works a man is justified, and not by faith only" (James 2:24). It in no way contradicts what the apostle Paul teaches when he said, "Therefore we conclude that a man is justified by faith without the deeds of the law" (Romans 3:28).

The explanation is evident. The works done by the converted Christian, to which the apostle James refers, occur as a product of faith. He does not do them to earn salvation, which comes only as a gift from Christ, but as the natural response of the human heart touched by the power of the Holy Spirit.

While our faith in Jesus and His priceless sacrifice form the basis of our salvation, it is also absolutely true that the fruits of obedience follow the authentic faith. If the faith is not capable of producing a change in life, it is not saving faith at all. It is not a covenant with God, a complete surrender to Him.

To present it in the inspired words of Ellen White: "While good works will not save even one soul, yet it is impossible for even one soul to be saved without good works" (1SM 377). While works do not have any value in themselves when done for the purpose of accumulating merits to earn salvation, they are the natural result of saving faith, which operates by love and transforms the heart. One of the best definitions of perfect faith is "surrender of self to God" (GW 260). "Saving faith is a transaction, by which those who receive Christ join themselves in covenant relation with God" (GW 261).

The imputed righteousness of Christ leads necessarily to imparted righteousness, which is nothing else but the process of spiritual growth and maturation, victory over sin. It results from the same faith and by the same power that brought justification. The great difference is that while we obtain justification immediately and must receive it over and over again, sanctification is an endless process, the work of a whole life. It continues in the experience of the child of God until the end of his earthly life.

In order for sanctification to take place "and in order for man to retain justification, there must be continual obedience, through active, living faith that works by love and purifies the soul" (1SM 366). John the Baptist referred to the indispensable works that follow true repentance and justification when he said, "Bring forth therefore fruits meet for repentance" (Matthew 3:8).

We are saved by grace through faith alone, but it is through "faith which worketh by love" (Galatians 5:6) and produces good works.

No better and clearer definition of the double character of the righteousness of Christ exists than the short one we find in *Messages to Young People*, page 35. "The righteousness by which we are justified is imputed; the righteousness by which we are sanctified is imparted. The first is our title to heaven, the second is our fitness for heaven." Both aspects of the righteousness of Christ are interrelated, and both are mutually indispensable. There is no possibility of justification without works that show the genuineness of our faith. On the other hand, till the end of the time of grace, there is no possibility of imparted righteousness, or sanctification, without constant dependence on the mercy, the sacrifice, and the life and death of Christ, and on His imputed righteousness. Many times even the good works that we may consider part of the imparted righteousness, though they're prompted by faith and as a response to love, are defective and tainted with selfishness. Moreover, our human nature continues to be sinful. Consequently, imputed righteousness has to come to aid and make effectual even the imparted righteousness.

The apostle John describes the whole process: "My little children, these things write I unto you, that ye sin not. And if any man sin, we have an advocate with the Father, Jesus Christ the righteous: and he is the propitiation for our sins" (1 John 2:1, 2). God's program for His children is that they do not sin after forgiveness, that they overcome sin. But our condition continues to be weak and subject to sin. Jesus stands ready to propitiate for our sins as long as we remain in the experience of repentance and recognition of our need and depend on Him for spiritual cleansing.

Some present the case of the thief on the cross as an example of imputed righteousness without a practical demonstration of its genuineness. But we should remember that the justified thief, the one that received from Christ the assurance of his salvation, rebuked the other malefactor for his lack of repentance, showing his faith through his works (words in this case) even on the cross.

The same apostle that Christianity considers the champion of justification by faith, in his great Epistle to the Romans, devotes many passages to show that justification cannot take place without a simultaneous and subsequent process of sanctification. Note the following scriptures: Romans 6:1-8, 11-14, 16; 7:1, 15-22; 8:1-10. Also, in the second part of his book Paul dedicates whole chapters, such as 12, 13, and 14, to the sanctified life that God expects from those justified by faith.

rinciple of Dependence and Cooperation

ngoing discussion continues among some people as to whether the power of God or the human part counts more in the plan of salvation and in the Christian life. Some overemphasize man's part. By doing so they end up in righteousness by works and legalism. Others overstress the absolute futility of the human part and state that God does the whole work. But that often results in a life devoid of the fruits of the Spirit. Nevertheless the Bible and Ellen White clearly disclose a divine plan of dependence and cooperation.

In spite of the gospel provisions, God cannot save or prepare for heaven any person not willing to do his or her part—in acquiescing and surrendering to God. Insignificant though it may seem, man's response is indispensable. That is why we find numerous expressions such as: "Choose life" (Deuteronomy 30:19); "Come unto me . . . [and] take my yoke" (Matthew 11:28, 29); "He that is not with me is against me" (Matthew 12:30); "If any man . . . open the door, I will come in" (Revelation 3:20); "Buy of me gold" (Revelation 3:18); "Enter ye in at the strait gate" (Matthew 7:13).

Suppose a man has fallen into a deep ditch from which he has no possibility of getting out by his own efforts. His cries for help attract the attention of someone, who lowers a large basket with a strong rope. The only thing the desperate victim needs to do is to step into the basket and take hold of the rope. But suppose he refuses to do so. To what avail is the equipment of the rescuer and his sincere desire to help the hopeless person? Only when the man in the ditch accepts the provision and puts his will into action, only when he steps into the basket, can his rescuer pull him out.

Cooperation With the Divine

Ellen White expresses the principle of our dependence on, and cooperation with, the divine in many beautiful passages. Speaking about what happened with Daniel, she said, "While God was working in Daniel and his companions 'to will and to do of his good pleasure,' they were working out their own salvation (Philippians 2:13). Herein is revealed the outworking of the divine principle of cooperation, without which no true success can be attained. Human effort avails nothing without divine power; and without human endeavor, divine effort is with many of no avail. To make God's grace our own, we must act our part. His grace is given to work in us to will and to do, but never as a substitute for our effort" (PK 486, 487).

Again, "For all created beings there is the one great principle of life—dependence upon and cooperation with God" (6T 236).

"God wishes us to have the mastery over ourselves. But He cannot help us without our consent and cooperation. The divine Spirit works through the powers and faculties given to man. Of ourselves we are not able to bring the purposes and desires and inclinations into harmony with the will of God; but if we are 'willing to be made willing,' the Saviour will accomplish this for us, 'casting down imaginations, and every high thing that exalteth itself against the knowledge of God, and bringing into captivity every thought to the obedience of Christ' (2 Corinthians 10:5)" (AA 482, 483).

Let us now consider the following inspired statements. We will not comment on them for lack of space:

"Man must work with his human power, aided by the divine power of Christ, to resist and to conquer at any cost to himself. In short, man must overcome as Christ overcame. . . . This could not be the case if Christ alone did all the overcoming. Man must do *his* part" (4T 32, 33, emphasis in original).

"Man needs a power out of and above himself to restore him to the likeness of God; but because he needs divine aid, it does not make human activity unessential. Faith on the part of man is required; for faith works by love and purifies the soul. Faith lays hold upon the virtue of Christ. The Lord does not design that human power should be paralyzed; but by cooperating with God, the power of man may be efficient for good. God does not design that our will should be destroyed; for it is through this very attribute that we are to accomplish the work He would have us to do" (1SM 375, 376).

"As the will of man cooperates with the will of God, it becomes omnipotent. Whatever is to be done at His command may be accomplished in His strength. All His biddings are enablings" (COL 333).

Here we find the divine formula for victory over sin.

"Let no man present the idea that man has little or nothing to do in the great work of overcoming; for God does nothing for man without his cooperation. Neither say that after you have done all you can on your part, Jesus will help you" (1SM 381).

"The Lord does not propose to perform for us either the willing or the doing. His grace is given to work in us to will and to do, but never as a substitute for our effort" (MYP 147).

Our hardest task is to submit to the will of God, yet it is something that we must do every step of the way. Self, urged on by Satan, unremittingly tries to prevent us from doing so. We do not need to choose deliberately to be against God. The minute we relax our determination to surrender to Jesus we give the enemy an advantage and place ourselves under his dominion.

Constantly we need to feel our need of God, to exercise our power of choice in order to put ourselves on God's side and allow Him to work in our behalf. Only then will the divine principle of dependence and cooperation bring forth its fruits of victory.

Partakers of the Divine Nature

If God's plan for us is to go and sin no more, He should have made ample provision to achieve this goal. Scriptures like 2 Peter 1:4; Jude 24; Ephesians 5:26, 27; and many more assure us that we can attain the plan of God through His strength. But it will take painstaking efforts and a constant active interest and cooperation on our part.

"A noble character is earned by individual effort through the merits and grace of Christ. God gives the talents, the powers of the mind; we form the character. It is formed by hard, stern battles with self. Conflict after conflict must be waged against hereditary tendencies. We shall have to criticize ourselves closely, and allow not one unfavorable trait to remain uncorrected" (COL 331).

"The Saviour's life of obedience maintained the claims of the law; it proved that the law could be kept in humanity, and showed the excellence of character that obedience would develop" (DA 309).

In spite of Satan's claim, many of God's children, through the grace of Christ, have reached the blessed goal of perfect obedience. The people of God who will be sealed and pass through the time of trouble also will attain that level of sanctification. They will be a great mass demonstration that the accusation of Satan against God was false.

"If we consent, He will so identify Himself with our thoughts and aims, so blend our hearts and minds into conformity to His will, that when obeying Him we shall be but carrying out our own impulses" (DA 668).

How to Secure Christ's Righteousness

As a summary of man's part in God's beautiful plan for the transformation of character and the reception of the imparted righteousness of Christ, let us briefly remember the following principles:

There should be a crucifixion of the old nature, a denial of self, even a dying of self. "If any man will come after me," said Jesus, "let him deny himself, and take up his cross, and follow me" (Matthew 16:24). And Galatians 2:20 conveys the same great principle: "I am crucified with Christ: nevertheless I live; yet not I, but Christ liveth in me." The ego does not reign anymore, for the person has been crucified with Christ, and in his stead, Christ rules and lives in him. But his life would have no room for the Master if self still dominated him.

The principle is similar to surrender. James teaches, "Submit yourselves therefore to God" (4:7). The verb *submit* is equivalent to surrender. "By His perfect obedience," Ellen White wrote, "He has made it possible for every human being to obey God's commandments. When we submit ourselves to Christ, the heart is united with His heart, the will is merged in His will, the mind becomes one with His mind, the thoughts are brought into captivity to Him; we live His life. This is what it means to be clothed with the garment of His righteousness" (COL 312).

"It is for you to yield up your will to the will of Jesus Christ; and as you do this, God will immediately take possession and work in you to will and to do of His good pleasure. Your whole nature will then be brought under the control of the Spirit of Christ, and even your thoughts will be subject to Him. You cannot control your impulses, your emotions, as you may desire; but you can control the will, and you can make an entire change in your life. By yielding up your will to Christ, your life will be hid with Christ in God and allied to the power which is above all principalities and powers. You will have strength from God that will hold you fast to His strength; and a new light, even the light of living faith, will be possible to you. But your will must cooperate with God's will" (Ellen G. White, *Our High Calling,* p. 103).

After our surrender, a wonderful miracle takes place: "When the soul surrenders itself to Christ, a new power takes possession of the new heart. A change is wrought which man can never accomplish for himself. . . . The soul that is yielded to Christ becomes His own fortress, . . . impregnable to the assaults of Satan" (DA 324).

But the fight of the Christian is not only a passive one. It is an active warfare. In the above-mentioned verse James continues, "Submit yourselves therefore to God. *Resist* the devil, and he will flee from you." Jesus did this, and Satan fled from Him.

Paul struggled daily. "His will and his desires every day conflicted with duty and the will of God. Instead of following inclination, he did God's will, however crucifying to his nature" (MH 452, 453).

Mrs. White tells us that "those who are waiting to behold a magical change in their characters without determined effort on their part to overcome sin, will be disappointed" (1SM 336, 337).

Naturally we should have a continual experience of repentance, confession, and putting away of sin. If done, and the promises of God claimed by faith in fervent prayer, then "every temptation, every opposing influence, whether open or secret, may be successfully resisted, 'not by might, nor by power, but by My spirit, saith the Lord of hosts' " (RH March 22, 1887).

And finally, we should ever keep open and use the lines of communication with heaven. We should spend time alone with God to receive strength for spiritual victory, to be endowed with the power of the Holy Spirit every day.

The righteousness of Christ will then be a beautiful experience in our life. We will live a happy life in peace with God and men, our hearts full of God's love, and we will have divine power at our command to overcome sin and to live victoriously.

Chapter 6

The Sealing

One of the most outstanding spiritual processes going on within the church today is the sealing. A spiritual operation God intends for the Holy Spirit to perform in each individual life as well as collectively in the whole church, it prepares us for the end of probationary time and the beginning of the time of trouble.

The level of character development that God's children need to have in order to receive the seal of the living God the following passage makes clear: "Those who receive the seal of the living God and are protected in the time of trouble must reflect the image of Jesus fully" (EW 71). "Not one of us will ever receive the seal of God while our characters have one spot or stain upon them" (5T 214).

So sobering is the thought that some have concluded that only a chosen few will be able to achieve it. But we have no reason to adopt such a defeatist attitude. The sealing is an actual and blessed possibility for everyone. God never requires from us anything impossible by His grace. The higher the goal and the harder the task, the closer our Father comes to each one of us and the greater the power He gives us. All His commands are enablings (COL 333). The imputed righteousness of Christ contains ample provision for our needs, so we can come boldly to God and ask for forgiveness and cleansing. There is enough power in the "exceeding great and precious promises: that by these ye might be partakers of the divine nature, having escaped the corruption that is in the world through lust" (2 Peter 1:4).

We receive three immediate consequences and

blessings through the sealing: (1) It so enshrines in the heart the principles of heaven and the commandments of God that in time of bitter persecution it gives steadfastness and loyalty, and in the time of trouble provides the saints protection from every sin and temptation. (2) It preserves the redeemed through the seven last plagues and also shields them by the power of God against physical damage in time of hardship and persecution. (3) It enables the sealed to see the King in His glory and to go to heaven with Him.

"Till We Have Sealed the Servants of Our God"

John the revelator withdraws the curtain in Revelation and allows us to watch an exciting scene that has a tremendous influence over the developments of the last days. He "saw four angels standing on the four corners of the earth, holding the four winds of the earth, that the wind should not blow on the earth, nor on the sea, nor on any tree. And I saw another angel ascending from the east, having the seal of the living God: and he cried with a loud voice to the four angels, to whom it was given to hurt the earth and the sea, saying, Hurt not the earth, neither the sea, nor the trees, till we have sealed the servants of our God in their foreheads. And I heard the number of them which were sealed: and there were sealed an hundred and forty and four thousand of all the tribes of the children of Israel" (Revelation 7:1-4).

Ellen White comments on what happens while the sealing takes place. "Four mighty angels hold back the powers of this earth till the servants of God are sealed in their foreheads. The nations of the world are eager for conflict; but they are held in check by the angels. When this restraining power is removed, there will come a time of trouble and anguish. . . .

"Angels are belting the world, refusing Satan his claims to supremacy, made because of the vast multitude of his adherents. We hear not the voices, we see not with the natural sight the work of these angels, but their hands are linked about the world, and with sleepless vigilance they are keeping the armies of Satan at bay till the sealing of

God's people shall be accomplished" (7BC 967).

The angels restrain the winds of strife, war, destruction, and human passions because the sealing of the servants of the Lord is being done.

In the days of Ezekiel the Lord commanded, "Go through the midst of the city, through the midst of Jerusalem, and set a mark upon the foreheads of the men that sigh and that cry for all the abominations that be done in the midst thereof" (Ezekiel 9:4). Today God will seal His people with a mark that will protect them during the time of trouble.

As we can see in Revelation 7:4, only those belonging to the group called the 144,000 will be sealed and will go triumphantly through the anguish of the last hour because they are fully prepared, and through the strength of God they have acquired the character needed for translation.

What the Seal of God Is

More than once the Bible uses the word *seal* to signify a mark of identification, such as with Abraham, of whom the apostle Paul said that "he received the sign of circumcision, a seal of the righteousness of the faith" (Romans 4:11). Circumcision was the external indication of an inner experience, "the righteousness of the faith."

Likewise, when we speak of the seal of the living God that He will place on the forehead of those who will be saved, we refer to an external evidence representing something that has happened in the inner being and life of the child of God.

In common language a seal could be both an instrument to place a mark and the mark itself left after one uses the material instrument on a document. The seal conceived as an instrument is the law of God, which, when applied by the Holy Spirit to our life and written on the fleshy tables of our heart (2 Corinthians 3:3; Hebrews 8:10; Ephesians 1:13; 4:30), changes our nature and causes our thoughts, words, feelings, desires, and ideals to come into agreement with the will of God expressed in His perfect law.

The fourth commandment gives the name of the Lawgiver, His title, His authority, and His territory. Ellen

White wrote that "the fourth commandment is the only one of all the ten in which are found both the name and the title of the Lawgiver. It is the only one that shows by whose authority the law is given. Thus it contains the seal of God, affixed to His law as evidence of its authenticity and binding force" (PP 307).

The Lord ordered Moses to speak to the children of Israel, "Verily my sabbaths ye shall keep: for it is a sign between me and you throughout your generations; that ye may know that I am the Lord that doth sanctify you" (Exodus 31:13). Sabbathkeeping was a mark or sign or seal of sanctification in the past, and it continues to have the same meaning today till the end.

But also a seal is a mark left on a document. That mark is first an evidence of authenticity. It means that the authority whose signature appears thereon wrote and signed it. In the same way, when the Holy Spirit seals a person, the power of Christ authentically transforms him, and he is now a child of God prepared for eternity. God has transferred or imparted the perfection of His character manifested in His law to his life, and he now reflects the image of his Father.

Also a seal is a symbol of ownership. As a sealed document belongs with all certainty to its owner, a child of God belongs to God his Father and to Christ his Saviour and Master. I still remember that when I was a boy we had to seal certified letters. The sender melted sealing wax on the envelope, and while the wax was still warm, he pressed his metal seal to it. The wax then would reproduce the characters or symbols on the seal.

Likewise, when the Holy Spirit applies the heavenly seal of God, His law of perfection—a reflection of His divine character—to our life, if the wax of our heart is warm and receptive—our human part—it will take exactly the shape of the original, and our life will bear the same perfect image of God.

The sealing process is nothing else than our sanctification, the transfer made by the power of God of the perfect character of Jesus to our own life, so that the imparted righteousness of Christ becomes a real experience.

And naturally, the seal should be also a sign of God's approval of our life. He considers us His property, and consequently He cares for us. At the same time it is a sign of loyalty on our part toward God our Owner and Christ our Lord and Redeemer.

Naturally Sabbathkeeping has meaning only to the extent in which it signifies what happened in our life, as baptism has meaning in the degree to which, as an external demonstration, it symbolizes the inner experience of the death of the old nature, crucified with Christ, and the resurrection of a new creature, risen to walk in newness of life. In other words, "not all who profess to keep the Sabbath will be sealed" (5T 213).

"What is the seal of the living God, which is placed in the foreheads of His people?" Mrs. White asks. "It is a mark which angels, but not human eyes, can read; for the destroying angel must see this mark of redemption" (4BC 1161). Why is it that human eyes cannot see it? Because it is nothing less than a character developed in the likeness of God, "a mark of redemption."

The Time of the Sealing

Chapter 7 of Revelation tells us that while the four angels hold the winds of strife and violence, the sealing angel performs his important mission. That means that the sealing is going on right now and that when the probationary time ends and the time of trouble begins, the sealing will have been finished.

Nobody knows how long the four angels will restrain chaos. But Ellen White does say, "The sealing time is very short, and will soon be over" (EW 58). Now we must develop in our characters the qualities and traits of the 144,000 (Revelation 14:4, 5). Only then will we be prepared for the time when God will withdraw His divine mercy from a wicked humanity.

A Process of Sanctification and Preparation

Ellen White defined the sealing as "a settling into the truth, both intellectually and spiritually, so they cannot be moved" (4BC 1161). In other words it is a process of sanctification and spiritual maturation. God's sealed people are so established in relationship with Christ that nothing can move them. No false doctrine or deception will deviate them from their experiential knowledge of the Word of God. No persecution will intimidate them or separate them from God. They will maintain absolute loyalty in face of ridicule, imprisonment, affliction, and death.

Only the Holy Spirit can produce such a miracle in our life. Paul teaches, "Grieve not the holy Spirit of God, whereby ye are sealed unto the day of redemption." "Ye were sealed with that holy Spirit of promise" (Ephesians 4:30; 1:13).

It is not something that we can postpone, an operation that can be effected instantaneously during crisis. Sanctification, the sealing, is an experience that we need to acquire throughout a life of self-denial, surrender to Christ, and daily obedience to God's will. While the Spirit still works in our behalf we should respond moment by moment.

Conditions for the Sealing

The only ones that will be sealed at the time of the end of the investigative judgment are the 144,000: "I heard the number of them which were sealed: and there were sealed an hundred and forty and four thousand of all the tribes of the children of Israel" (Revelation 7:4).

In my companion book, *The Impending Drama*, I devoted a major part of one chapter to the 144,000. Here I would like to review their characteristics. (1) They are redeemed from the earth (Revelation 14:3). The blood of the Lamb purchased them, and they accepted the call to be children of God, separated from the world. (2) They are sealed (Revelation 7:4). They have obtained victory over sin and weaknesses of character. Their hearts bear the imprint of God's law. (3) The name of the Father is "written in their foreheads" (Revelation 14:1). They belong to the family of God, completely identified in their thoughts, feelings, words, and actions with the things of heaven. (4) Not defiled with women, they are virgins (verse 4). They have not accepted false doctrines or engaged in activities that conflict with the Word of God. (5) "In their mouth was found no guile" (verse 5). They are truthful in all their dealings. Deception does not find any place in their life. (6) "They are without fault" (verse 5), having reached the special level of sinlessness the children of God need to have at that time. No spot or wrinkle mars their character.

"Not one of us will ever receive the seal of God while our characters have one spot or stain upon them. . . . We are too easily satisfied with our attainments" (5T 214). "Those who receive the seal of the living God and are protected in the time of trouble must reflect the image of Jesus fully" (EW 71).

"Those that overcome the world, the flesh, and the devil, will be the favored ones who shall receive the seal of the living God. Those whose hands are not clean, whose hearts are not pure, will not have the seal of the living God. Those who are planning sin and acting it will be passed by. Only those who, in their attitude before God, are filling the position of those who are repenting and confessing their sins in the great antitypical day of atonement, will be recognized and marked as worthy of God's protection. The names of those who are steadfastly looking and waiting and watching for the appearing of their Saviour—more earnestly and wishfully than they who wait for the morning—will be numbered with those who are sealed. . . .

"Will this seal be put upon the impure in mind, the fornicator, the adulterer, the man who covets his neighbor's wife? Let your souls answer the question, Does my character correspond to the qualifications essential that I may receive a passport to the mansions Christ has prepared for those who are fitted for them? Holiness must be inwrought in our character" (TM 445, 446).

The Only Way of Reaching the Conditions

The conditions are so high that the enemy may put in our minds the idea that only a small select group of Christians will reach them. But Ephesians 1:13 rejects that idea. "In whom [Christ] also after that ye believed, ye were sealed with that holy Spirit of promise." In Christ and through the Holy Spirit all can receive the seal of God. Salvation is for everybody and not for just a few. It does not depend upon natural conditions or a privileged heredity.

"The grace of God has dawned upon the world with healing for all mankind," the apostle Paul said in Titus 2:11 (NEB*). Even the less privileged, the weakest, can receive forgiveness and cleansing through the imputed righteousness of Christ. Then, surrendering to Jesus and taking advantage of the means of grace God has provided, they can acquire the imparted character of Jesus and be ready for the sealing.

"The filthy garments are to be removed, and Christ's robe of righteousness is to be placed upon us. By repentance and faith we are enabled to render obedience to all the commandments of God, and are found without blame before Him. Those who shall meet the approval of God are now afflicting their souls, confessing their sins, and earnestly pleading for pardon through Jesus their Advocate" (5T 472).

We find complete assurance of success in a promise like Paul's: "Thanks be to God, which giveth us the victory through our Lord Jesus Christ" (1 Corinthians 15:57). Any one of us, no matter what his present condition, can reach the experience of Paul, who according to the last verses of Romans 7 felt all the desperation of somebody fighting against the law of sin inherent in human nature. He recognized his utter impotence, comparing himself with a miserable man chained to a corpse and left to die (Romans 7:5). But with absolute confidence he expresses the complete change effected in his life through Jesus: "The law of the Spirit of life in Christ Jesus hath made me free from the law of sin and death" (Romans 8:2).

And the assurance occurs again in Hebrews 7:25: "He [Christ] is able also to save them to the uttermost that come unto God by him, seeing he ever liveth to make intercession for them." Even the underprivileged, spiritually speaking, can reach that experience. Among the many promises of God we find one that gives us the certainty of achieving a blameless life through Christ: "Unto him that is

*From The New English Bible. Copyright, The Delegates of the Oxford University Press and The Syndics of the Cambridge University Press 1961, 1970. Reprinted by permission.

able to keep you from falling, and to present you faultless before the presence of his glory with exceeding joy" (Jude 24).

Ellen White adds her inspired testimony to Scripture's wonderful words of comfort and absolute certainty: "No one need say that his case is hopeless, that he cannot live the life of a Christian. Ample provision is made by the death of Christ for every soul. Jesus is our ever-present help in time of need. Only call upon Him in faith, and He has promised to hear and answer your petitions" (5T 215).

Chapter 7

The Holy Spirit

We begin in this chapter the study of a difficult subject, one we will never be able to fully explain—the mysterious nature, power, and operation of the Holy Spirit. But in Christian life this is not the important thing. What really matters is to experience His power that operates within and without man. His inward manifestation appears in our victory over all human weaknesses. The outward we see evidenced in the gospel presentation, which succeeds despite human limitations.

Although the Third Person of the Godhead has been always working for the restoration of man from sin, we live in a special time we can rightly call the age of the Spirit. "The dispensation in which we are now living is to be, to those that ask, the dispensation of the Holy Spirit" (TM 511). It began at Pentecost, and it will not end until God finishes His work in our world. The activity of the Holy Spirit will be more evident and more abundant than ever before, surpassing even Pentecost.

The same thing we said in our chapter on righteousness by faith has to be said about the Holy Spirit. Although on this side of heaven we may never fully understand the subject intellectually or theoretically, we should thoroughly know firsthand the presence and the power of the Spirit, and we should be witnesses of His activity in our life. In this respect the Holy Spirit is not a doctrine or a theory, but an experience, and until He becomes a living reality in our life, we will never catch the central importance of His work. Although I may not have a scientific knowledge of electricity, I should be able to know electrical power on a practical level because I use it every day and benefit from it.

The importance of the Holy Spirit in the work of the gospel appears in an often-repeated sentence, "This promised blessing, claimed by faith, brings all other blessings in its train" (GW 285). So the promise of Christ to send Him takes a special relevancy and a tremendous meaning in our preparation for the final events and the coming of the Lord.

The Godhead: a Perfect Unity

The nature of the Holy Trinity, which is just one God (1 Timothy 2:5) but manifested in three different personalities—God the Father, God the Son, and God the Holy Spirit—is a mystery that no one can explain and no man can fully understand. The use in several Hebrew passages of the Old Testament word *Elohim,* which is a plural noun—Gods—but coupled with a singular verb, reflects the plurality of persons that makes the Godhead but the absolute unity of the three of them.

No illustration can adequately explain the Trinity, because we know of nothing similar to it in human experience or even in nature. The distinction of the three persons and at the same time the fact that they comprise just one God we observe in such scriptures as the gospel commission Christ gave, where He said, "Go ye therefore, and teach all nations, baptizing them in the name of the Father, and of the Son, and of the Holy Ghost" (Matthew 28:19). Also we find it in expressions of the apostle Paul, who wrote, "The grace of the Lord Jesus Christ, and the love of God, and the communion of the Holy Ghost, be with you all" (2 Corinthians 13:14). The unity and intimate cooperation between the three persons manifested itself in the baptism of Christ. When emerging from the water, "he saw the Spirit of God descending like a dove, and lighting upon him: and lo a voice from heaven, saying, This is my beloved Son, in whom I am well pleased" (Matthew 3:16, 17).

In the same way as the three persons cooperated in the event of Christ's baptism, they work together with absolute unity to apply the atoning work of Christ to every saved person. The three are present in the justification of man, in the regeneration of the heart, in sanctification, and in the communication of God effected by His children to sinners.

The three persons are actively engaged in saving men. "The Godhead was stirred with pity for the race, and the Father, the Son, and the Holy Spirit gave themselves to the working out of the plan of redemption" (CH 222). Normally we think about the Son of God giving Himself for man's redemption. But the three members of the Godhead are so united that truly the three of them are just one God, and actually they gave themselves, because God the Father suffered in the person of His Son, and so did the Holy Spirit.

In another clear paragraph Ellen White wrote: "The Father, the Son, and the Holy Spirit, the three holy dignitaries of heaven, have declared that they will strengthen men to overcome the powers of darkness. All the facilities of heaven are pledged to those who by their baptismal vows have entered into a covenant with God" (5BC 1110).

"There are three living persons of the heavenly trio; in the name of these three great powers—the Father, the Son, and the Holy Spirit—those who receive Christ by living faith are baptized, and these powers will cooperate with the obedient subjects of heaven in their efforts to live the new life in Christ" (Ev 615).

Each one of the members of the Trinity is fully God and has in Him all the divine qualities and characteristics. The three of them are one in thought, in plans, in action, and in their love for and interest in humanity. Every one of them is holy, every one is omnipotent, eternal, and omniscient.

An Individual Personality

The Bible does not speak of the Holy Spirit as an impersonal power or an influence, as some people like to think. The different verbs applied by the Bible writers to the work of the Spirit do not fit with the concept of an impersonal force.

For example, Romans 15:30 speaks about "the love of the Spirit." A mere influence or power cannot love. Only a person can. The Greek expression, when translated literally, means "for the love that the Spirit has." The Spirit speaks (1 Timothy 4:1); reproves (John 16:8); teaches (John

14:26). We may insult and sin against Him (Hebrews 10:29; Matthew 12:31, 32). Paul talks about having communion with Him (2 Corinthians 13:14).

Several quotations used previously declare the same thing, and we could add even more. "The prince of the power of evil can only be held in check by the power of God in the third person of the Godhead, the Holy Spirit" (Ev 617). At a meeting in the Avondale College in Australia, Ellen White made a statement she later wrote in a letter: "We need to realize that the Holy Spirit, who is as much a person as God is a person, is walking through these grounds" (Ev 616, from MS 66, 1899).

So our relationship with God and with Christ, through the Holy Spirit who abides in us, is really more like a human and warm relationship. We do not deal with a mysterious force but with a Person who loves us and is as much at work for our salvation as the Father and the Son. At the same time we should keep in mind that He can help us only to the extent in which we fulfill the conditions for His indwelling and in which we cooperate with Him. The best way to cooperate is to obey Him and do the things that He impresses us to do. Otherwise we would be quenching the Spirit, grieving Him, obligating Him to leave.

Representative of God and Christ

One of the main missions of the Spirit is to represent God and Christ in our lives. "He shall not speak of himself," said Christ; "but whatsoever he shall hear, that shall he speak" (John 16:13). "I will pray the Father, and he shall give you another Comforter, that he may abide with you for ever" (John 14:16).

Mrs. White tells us that "Christ is represented by the Holy Spirit; and when this Spirit is appreciated, when those controlled by the Spirit communicate to others the energy with which they are imbued, an invisible chord is touched which electrifies the whole" (6BC 1053).

"He [the seeker of truth] prays for the Holy Spirit, the representative of Christ, to be his constant guide" (CT 450). Jesus called Him "the Comforter, which is the Holy Ghost, whom the Father will send in my name" (John 14:26). Sent by the Father in the name of Jesus, the Spirit represents both the Father and the Son, abiding in man to guide him, teach him, comfort him, purify him, and give him power to win against evil and sin.

Should the disciples have continued to enjoy the literal companionship of the Master, they would not have felt their need of the Holy Spirit's presence. When Christ was in person among men, His human form limited Him to benefiting only a certain group of persons at a time. But once He ascended to heaven and sent His Spirit, He could be in closer contact with His disciples regardless of time and space, since the Spirit could be everywhere at the same time and still take care of every individual's need as if he were the only one in the world. In other words, the ministry of the Spirit extends the presence of God and of Christ everywhere at any time.

Only through the ministry of the Spirit could the counsel "Abide in me, and I in you" be a reality. And "through the Spirit the believer becomes a partaker of the divine nature. Christ has given His Spirit as a divine power to overcome all hereditary and cultivated tendencies to evil, and to impress His own character upon His church" (DA 671).

Functions of the Holy Spirit

1. John 16:8 describes the most basic work of the Spirit of God: "He will reprove the world of sin, and of righteousness, and of judgment." The Greek verb for "reprove" means also "convict," "convince." If it were not for the Holy Spirit and His influence on the sinner's heart, no one would be able to experience repentance or to feel sadness for having broken the law of God and to feel the desire to abandon sin. Man finds no merit in his repentance, because it is something prompted by the Holy Spirit.

The Spirit is always pleading and convincing the individual heart about his spiritual needs. When the heart responds to His tender voice, repentance, confession, forgiveness, and peace follow in consequence.

Not only does the Spirit work in the heart of the Christian but also in everybody's heart. He leads the murderer, the drunkard, the robber to conversion. Because of Him, man recognizes his selfishness, his pride, his covetousness, his worldliness, his intemperance, his bad temper and impatience, or other defects of character, and he feels a longing to be liberated from his weakness.

Also the Spirit convicts human hearts of the need for righteousness, conveying to them, through the help of the Word of God or through some messenger, the imputed and the imparted righteousness of Christ, leading them to the Saviour.

Christ said that the Spirit also would speak about the judgment. The conviction that every person will have to appear in judgment in the courts of heaven arouses in many a sense of responsibility and a desire to accept the salvation Jesus offers.

2. John 14:26 and 16:13 describe another function of the Holy Spirit: to teach, to guide into all truth, and to bring all the things we have studied back to our remembrance.

Some churches claim the infallible mastership (teachership) of the church, but the only infallible teachership mentioned in the Bible is that of the Holy Spirit, the Unerrant Teacher. When we open the Sacred Book with reverence and with a prayer that He will lead us into all truth in fulfillment of the promise, He opens our mind to the understanding of the great principles of the gospel.

But He is no substitute for deep study and hard work. Actually what the Spirit does is to reward those who dig deep into the inexhaustible mine of truth found in the Bible, with new revelations and new insights, preventing them from falling into false concepts and errors. They must, of course, approach the study and meditation of the Word with a teachable spirit and an open mind. And God sends His Spirit only to those who obey Him.

The discovery of truth will not come all at once but rather little by little. The pioneers of the Adventist movement in the first days of our history reached a full grasp of some of the basic doctrines of the Word only over an extended period of time.

It is interesting to find that the Spirit not only leads us into truth but also brings items we have previously studied back into our consciousness. When we study the Word under His leadership, although the memory of some truth may slip out of our conscious mind, He can retrieve it even from our subconscious at the right moment we need it, whether it be in a talk or a moment of crisis or emergency. The daily study of the Holy Book will equip our mind with the promise, the instructions, the reproof, or the knowledge we need to assure our preparation for eternity.

3. A third function of the Spirit has to do with our prayers. Prayer is one of the basic elements for a successful Christian life. It keeps the channels of communication open to heaven. Along with faith it offers to us the infinite resources of God.

The problem is that "we know not what we should pray for as we ought." But "the Spirit itself maketh intercession for us . . . according to the will of God" (Romans 8:26, 27). So not only the Father and the Son involve themselves in our prayers—for Jesus says, "Whatsoever ye shall ask in my name that will I do, that the Father may be glorified in the Son" (John 14:13)—but also the Holy Spirit, who, knowing the will of God for us, sends on to heaven those prayers of ours, made perfect and acceptable in the sight of God. Hence, we should not lose our faith or get discouraged if we do not receive the things we ask for, because they may not be for our good. But always our Father hears and answers our prayers, sometimes sending us what we need most.

Also we should not be disappointed if God does not send us the blessing we request, even though it may be according to the will of God, like the conversion of a son or a parent. In conversion the Spirit has to work little by little because He cannot impose His presence on any unwilling heart. But somehow the Lord will continue to influence the individual, perhaps shaking that life with strange trials to arouse the conscience and enlist the will. The Lord may even delay His answer in order to deepen the person's interest, strengthen his faith, and make more fervent his prayer. Thus He teaches us how to persevere and humbly throw the weight of our longing on Him, saying, "I will not let thee go, except thou bless me" (Genesis 32:26).

4. Romans 8:16 contains a fourth mission of the Spirit.

"The Spirit itself beareth witness with our spirit, that we are the children of God." How comforting to know without a shadow of doubt that God has accepted us as children, that He has covered us with the perfect robe of righteousness, and that He guides, especially when the fog of discouragement surrounds us and the enemy wants to make us feel disappointed.

"The Holy Spirit is a person, for He beareth witness with our spirits that we are the children of God. When this witness is borne, it carries with it its own evidence. At such times we believe and are sure that we are the children of God" (Ev 616).

5. One of the most wonderful consequences of the Spirit's abiding in our heart is the fruit He produces (Galatians 5:22, 23). It comprises an amazing array of Christian virtues. We cannot engender any one of them by human effort. Their appearance is a miracle done by the Spirit.

"The life-giving power of the Holy Spirit, proceeding from the Saviour, pervades the soul, renews the motives and affections, and brings even the thoughts into obedience to the will of God, enabling the receiver to bear the precious fruit of holy deeds" (AA 284).

Jesus told Nicodemus, "Except a man be born of water and of the Spirit, he cannot enter into the kingdom of God" (John 3:5). The Holy Spirit brings about the new birth. He transforms the life, changes the thoughts and feelings, puts new desires, new tastes, and new ideals in the heart, keeps the thoughts pure and holy, and sanctifies the emotions.

The Presence of the Spirit in Our Life

But all such spiritual benefits come only if man allows the Spirit to work in him. The Spirit can function only if permitted to dwell in the heart.

In this sense our bodies and minds become "the temple of God," so that "the Spirit of God dwelleth in . . . [us]" (1 Corinthians 3:16). The mysterious and dynamic work of the Spirit is a miracle that no science or psychology can explain.

Not long ago I attended a lecture of a learned scholar and psychologist. Drawing a diagram on the blackboard, he claimed to be able to explain through the laws of psychology the transformation made by the gospel. At the end of his elaborate one-hour presentation I had to tell him that according to the Bible the work of the Holy Spirit in human life is a mystery that supersedes science and psychology, and it cannot be explained by science or be contained within the scope of any set of so-called psychological laws.

Nevertheless, although a mystery to the human mind, even of the scientist's and of the scholar's, it is a wonderful operation that the born-again child of God is completely familiar with because he has gone through the process.

In spite of God's eager willingness to endow His children with the Holy Spirit's beneficent power (Luke 11:13), many a Christian walks through life without it because he is not willing to fulfill the conditions, since according to an inspired statement, "it is given . . . according to the capacity to receive" (DA 672).

The opening of the heart (Revelation 3:20), the request for the Spirit (Luke 11:13) in fervent supplication, and especially the denial of self (Mark 8:34) and its surrender to Christ are the most basic conditions to receive "this promised blessing, claimed by faith," that "brings all other blessings in its train" (DA 672).

Chapter 8

Stages in the Work of the Holy Spirit

A throng of anxious people, crowded into the Temple, pressed together to hear Peter's sermon. Under the mighty impact of the Holy Spirit thousands of sincere men and women cried, "Men and brethren, what shall we do? Then Peter said unto them, Repent, and be baptized every one of you in the name of Jesus Christ for the remission of sins, and ye shall receive the gift of the Holy Ghost" (Acts 2:37, 38).

The reception of the gift of the Holy Spirit by the born-again Christian is a pivotal experience in his life. One cannot be a real child of God without enjoying the blessed presence of the Third Person of the Godhead. Today many people, unhappy and unsatisfied with their religious achievement, are looking for something new and more meaningful than the cold religion they are acquainted with. Satan has taken advantage of their interest and has caused the upsurge of movements that give a false meaning to such Biblical expressions as "filled with the Holy Ghost" or "baptized with the Holy Ghost."

Christ told His disciples, "John [the Baptist] truly baptized with water; but ye shall be baptized with the Holy Ghost not many days hence" (Acts 1:5). In this chapter we will study the different stages or operations in the work of the Holy Spirit on the human heart and the meaning of the baptism of the Spirit. Also we will see how it can be achieved and by whom.

One thing is sure. God desires that every one of His children may receive the fullness of the Spirit and may really know he has been baptized by the Heavenly Power. Right after the conversion of Paul on his way to Damascus, the Lord sent Ananias with an encouraging message: "The Lord . . . hath sent me, that thou mightest . . . be filled with the Holy Ghost" (Acts 9:17). God seeks to fill every one of His people with the Spirit.

The Lord generously bestows the heavenly goods necessary for our salvation. When Jesus speaks about spiritual life, He says, "I am come that they might have life, and that they might have it more abundantly" (John 10:10). After all, He is the Omnipotent One "that is able to do exceeding abundantly above all that we ask or think" (Ephesians 3:20). "God giveth not the Spirit by measure" (John 3:34) but lavishly.

A Convicting Power

The Lord works on the human heart through His Holy Spirit long before man has any desire for a holy life or any inclination toward religious matters. The promise of John 16:8—"And when he is come, he will reprove the world of sin, and of righteousness, and of judgment"—presents the Spirit of God as a convicting power. In the first stage or operation He speaks to non-Christians, to the nonreligious, as well as to individuals who have been children of God for a long time.

Using His quiet but effective language, the Spirit brings us face-to-face with the reality of sin, of righteousness, and of judgment. In other words the Spirit persuades man that he is a sinner, leads him to look for righteousness in Jesus, and admonishes him about the coming judgment to encourage repentance.

Speaking about the working of the Holy Spirit on human hearts, Ellen White wrote that "the Author of this spiritual life [the Holy Spirit, proceeding from the Saviour] is unseen, and the exact method by which that life is imparted and sustained, it is beyond the power of human philosophy to explain. Yet the operations of the Spirit are always in harmony with the written word" (AA 284).

About the Spirit's role in conviction, she said, "When the heart yields to the influence of the Spirit of God, the conscience will be quickened, and the sinner will discern something of the depth and sacredness of God's holy law. . . . Conviction takes hold upon the mind and heart. The sinner has a sense of the righteousness of Jehovah and feels the terror of appearing, in his own guilt and uncleanness, before the Searcher of hearts. He sees the love of God, the beauty of holiness, the joy of purity; he longs to be cleansed and to be restored to communion with Heaven" (SC 24).

Naturally, man can either respond to or refuse the call of the Spirit. But the latter choice grieves the Spirit (Ephesians 4:30). Nevertheless, He continues to plead over and over again, trying to soften the human heart, and He stops only when the person has hardened his heart to such an extent that he is no longer sensitive to His voice.

The process of conviction affects everybody. But the Spirit does not yet abide in the heart. Actually He works, in a sense, from the outside.

An Indwelling Power

The plan of God and the longing of the Spirit is that man reach the second stage, where the Spirit enters into the heart and dwells there. "I will pray the Father, and he shall give you another Comforter, that he may abide with you for ever. . . . He dwelleth with you, and shall be in you" (John 14:16, 17). God wants to make our person the permanent temple of the Holy Spirit. And when that happens, then the Spirit begins to change the life.

In speaking with Nicodemus, Jesus compared the action of the Spirit with that of the wind: "The wind bloweth where it listeth, and thou hearest the sound thereof, but canst not tell whence it cometh, and whither it goeth" (John 3:8). Despite its mysterious operation, we can clearly see results. Notwithstanding the fact that the work done by God through His Holy Spirit is as invisible as the wind, we readily notice its effects. After man surrenders his life to God, the Spirit begins spiritual renewal and transformation that Christ calls a new birth: "Except a man be born of water and of the Spirit, he cannot enter into the kingdom of God" (verse 5).

As soon as the first change occurs in the life and the

person becomes willing to obey His leading, the Spirit brings spiritual growth, and the fruit of the Spirit appears in that life (Galatians 5:22, 23).

The heart identifies more and more completely with Jesus. The growing Christian who more fully surrenders himself to God develops an increasing desire to obey Him and to give his life in a stronger commitment to the Lord. As the process continues, sanctification is more evident. Love replaces hatred and selfishness, joy takes away sadness and depression, peace abolishes anxiety and anguish, long-suffering displaces a dominant spirit and intolerance, gentleness erases roughness, goodness overcomes wickedness. Faith eradicates fear and insecurity, meekness eliminates arrogance and strife for position, and temperance, or self-control, gives stability to the whole life.

The growth not only shows up in the character but also in one's knowledge of the truth. As the Holy Spirit leads the person in his study of the Word (John 16:13; 14:26), he continues "increasing in the knowledge of God" (Colossians 1:10) and growing "in grace, and in the knowledge of our Lord and Saviour Jesus Christ" (2 Peter 3:18).

Since the Spirit brings with Him the indwelling presence of Jesus, we experience a purifying influence and a protection against sin. But we need to renew moment by moment our surrender to God and our relationship with Jesus, so that the Spirit may instill into us the life of the vine that causes us to flourish and bring forth rich fruits (John 15:1-7).

"It is by the Spirit that the heart is made pure. Through the Spirit the believer becomes a partaker of the divine nature. Christ has given His Spirit as a divine power to overcome all hereditary and cultivated tendencies to evil, and to impress His own character upon His church" (DA 671).

According to Revelation 3:20 only those who open the door, who respond to the calls of the Spirit, who consent for Christ to enter into their hearts, will benefit from His abiding presence. In other words, the permanence and the work of the Spirit in the heart depend on our will, our interest, and our fervent desire.

But there exists one danger. Once the Spirit has entered a person's life, He may leave again if the individual does not meet certain conditions. Paul admonishes us, "Grieve not the holy Spirit of God, whereby ye are sealed unto the day of redemption" (Ephesians 4:30). Our disinterest, our worldliness, our lack of communion with God, our disobedience, creates a situation that obliges Him to depart from us.

Realizing my absolute need, do I surrender every day so completely to Jesus and in faith and humility plead with God for the presence of His Spirit with such intensity as to warrant the permanence of God's Representative in my life?

Another great hurdle awaits the continuing presence of the Spirit in our heart: sin and self. "Each one will have a close struggle to overcome sin in his own heart. . . . Everyone who enters the pearly gates of the city of God will enter there as a conqueror, and his greatest conquest will have been the conquest of self" (9T 182, 183).

One of the greatest obstacles the Spirit must face is the unconverted hearts of some of His messengers. "If we would humble ourselves before God, and be kind and courteous and tenderhearted and pitiful, there would be one hundred conversions to the truth where now there is only one. But, though professing to be converted, we carry around with us a bundle of self that we regard as altogether too precious to be given up. It is our privilege to lay this burden at the feet of Christ and in its place take the character and similitude of Christ. The Saviour is waiting for us to do this" (9T 189, 190).

An Enabling Power

Christ's promise in Acts 1:5 reads: "John truly baptized with water; but ye shall be baptized with the Holy Ghost not many days hence." Now, from the Bible standpoint, to be baptized with the Holy Spirit does not imply any strange physical sensation or any unusual emotional condition that may lead to bodily contortions or to glossolalia. It simply means receiving in a quiet way the power that will enable us to testify for the Lord Jesus Christ.

ance that the whole world will be evangelized: "After these things I saw another angel come down from heaven, having great power; and the earth was lightened with his glory." The angel does not represent a new message, additional to those of Revelation 14, but a new power—the glory and the power of the Holy Spirit, which will make our witnessing effective.

Conditions for the Work of the Holy Spirit

Why is it that God's promises about the Holy Spirit, especially those that have to do with the latter rain, have not yet been completely fulfilled? It is simply because we as individuals and as a church have not met the conditions, or prerequisites, since the gift of the Spirit comes to us "according to the capacity to receive." "Like every other promise, it is given on conditions" (DA 672).

In summary, what are the conditions?

1. *To repent and confess sin* (Acts 2:38; 1 John 1:9). This is the gateway to Christian experience, fellowship with God, and reception of His Spirit. But we need to meet several other requisites in order to keep Him and to increase His power and influence in our lives.

2. *To ask for the Spirit daily* (Luke 11:13). We must long for His presence as we do for food and water when we are desperately hungry or thirsty.

3. *To obey the Spirit* (Acts 5:32). As soon as the Spirit enters our heart He wants to lead our life, to encourage us to do God's will, and to eliminate bad thoughts and habits. "We cannot use the Holy Spirit; the Spirit is to use us" (GW 285). And if He is to use us, we have to obey Him. Otherwise we will lose His presence.

4. *To be cleansed from all bad habits, sins, and destructive feelings that mar our spiritual life* (Ephesians 4:17-32). Verse 30 contains a development of the central idea of not grieving the Holy Spirit. The apostle explains to us how we may be cleansed, namely, by liberating ourselves from all kinds of sin through the strength of God.

5. *To witness for Christ.* God expects us to obey His Spirit in the matter of release from sin, bad habits, selfishness, greed, hatred, bitterness, and any other kind of

weakness. It applies in a special way to the proclamation of the gospel. Acts 1:8 tells us that the express reason why God gave us the Spirit is to help us bear witness for Christ.

6. *To renounce the ego and die to self* (Matthew 16:24). The denial of ourselves eliminates one of the hardest barriers against receiving or keeping the Spirit. "There is no limit to the usefulness of the one who, putting self aside, makes room for the working of the Holy Spirit upon his heart, and lives a life wholly consecrated to God" (ChS 254).

Self has many ways of manifesting itself: in pride, bitterness, hate, an unforgiving spirit, strife for supremacy. Unless we learn from Jesus how to have the same humble spirit He had, we cannot receive or keep the Spirit.

7. *To have faith* (Galatians 3:14). Many times the sense of our own sinfulness leaves us depressed, and the enemy prevents us from praying with faith and conviction. But we should remember that one of the functions of the Spirit is to cleanse us and to keep us from sin. God is more willing than any human father to bestow upon us His best gift. The secret of receiving is believing (Mark 11:24). When faith lays hold of God's promise, the Lord supplies the fact, not because of our own merits, but because, having none, we claim the promise in the name of Jesus and act accordingly.

A Daily Experience

We commit a great mistake when we associate receiving the fullness of the Spirit or being baptized by the Spirit with some spectacular phenomenon that happens once and for all time. That is not the case. It is rather something that should happen daily, in a quiet, subdued way, while we meditate on the Word of God and hear the voice of the Spirit talking to us personally.

In the same way our Lord was baptized anew every day by the Spirit. "From hours spent with God He came forth morning by morning, to bring the light of heaven to men. Daily He received a fresh baptism of the Holy Spirit" (COL 139). "Morning by morning, as the heralds of the gospel kneel before the Lord and renew their vows of consecration to Him, He will grant them the presence of His Spirit" (AA 56).

Chapter 9

The Early and the Latter Rain

It has always been God's plan to bestow His Holy Spirit abundantly, both to the individual believer and to the church at large. And when there exists a real thirst for that heavenly blessing, a sincere desire borne from a sense of need, the Lord fulfills His promises. Christ repeatedly expressed the Father's willingness to grant the gift. He said, "Blessed are they which do hunger and thirst after righteousness: for they shall be filled" (Matthew 5:6). "In the last day, that great day of the feast, Jesus stood and cried, saying, If any man thirst, let him come unto me, and drink. He that believeth on me, as the scripture hath said, out of his belly shall flow rivers of living water. (But this spake he of the Spirit, which they that believe on him should receive)" (John 7:37-39).

It should encourage us that when Jesus spoke about the bestowal of the Holy Spirit to the believer He used metaphors and symbols that conveyed the idea of plenitude, of richness, of overflowing.

God uses the illustration of the normal recurrence of the rain in the land of Palestine to explain His plan. The Lord's "going forth is prepared as the morning; and he shall come unto us as the rain, as the latter and former rain unto the earth" (Hosea 6:3). The former or early rain used to come in Eastern lands shortly after the sowing time. It caused the seed to germinate; whereas the latter rain fell shortly before the harvest, maturing the crop.

The outpouring of the early and the latter rain of the Holy Spirit refers not only to the concession of the Spirit to the individual Christian but also and especially to the church at large.

The Early Rain in the Historic Realm

The symbol of the early and the latter rain, therefore, has two different applications. Speaking about the church and its history, the early rain happened at Pentecost and the rest of the apostolic age, whereas the latter rain will occur during the last days in order to ripen the crop for the harvest.

At the same time the individual experience has an early and a latter rain. We will refer to this aspect later.

The prophet Joel, under the inspiration of God, wrote, "It shall come to pass afterward, that I will pour out my spirit upon all flesh; and your sons and your daughters shall prophesy, your old men shall dream dreams, your young men shall see visions: and also upon the servants and upon the handmaids in those days will I pour out my spirit" (Joel 2:28, 29).

Acts 2 relates the miraculous fulfillment of that prophecy: "When the day of Pentecost was fully come, they were all with one accord in one place. And suddenly there came a sound from heaven as of a rushing mighty wind, and it filled all the house where they were sitting. And there appeared unto them cloven tongues like as of fire, and it sat upon each of them. And they were all filled with the Holy Ghost, and began to speak with other tongues, as the Spirit gave them utterance" (verses 1-4).

The results of that outpouring of power, accompanied by the gift of tongues, appeared at the end of Peter's and the other apostles' presentation when everyone spoke a different language. "The Holy Spirit did for them that which they could not have accomplished for themselves in a lifetime" (AA 39, 40). So the disciples received, by virtue of the early rain of the Spirit, the final qualification they needed to accomplish their lifework. The new tongue that the Spirit gave them facility to handle they all used in such a way that their language was from that time on "pure, simple, and accurate," and their words found direct access to the inner recesses of the heart. Prejudices disappeared. The Spirit convicted men and women from different parts of the world, gathered in Jerusalem for the annual festivities, with the fact that the crucified Christ was the Son of God, the Messiah, that He was resurrected from the dead, and that He was able to give eternal salvation to all who accepted Him. Three thousand people received Jesus that same day, were baptized, and joined the rising church.

Not only was Palestine the scene of such miracles, but the glad news of the gospel shook the uttermost parts of the inhabited world. The work of the Spirit was so effective that many of those who at first were among the fiercest opponents of the gospel of Jesus became some of its most powerful promoters.

Promises of the Latter Rain

The prophecy of Joel (2:23, 28-31) about the outpouring of the Spirit had to have, according to the plans of God, two fulfillments. The first one was at Pentecost. The second and more abundant one was to be the latter rain. "Christ has promised the gift of the Holy Spirit to His church, and the promise belongs to us as much as to the first disciples" (DA 672).

In 1892 Mrs. White stated, "Today you are to have your vessel purified that it may be ready for the heavenly dew, ready for the showers of the latter rain; for the latter rain will come, and the blessing of God will fill every soul that is purified from every defilement. It is our work today to yield our souls to Christ, that we may be fitted for the time of refreshing from the presence of the Lord—fitted for the baptism of the Holy Spirit" (1SM 191).

"As the 'former rain' was given, in the outpouring of the Holy Spirit at the opening of the gospel, to cause the upspringing of the precious seed, so the 'latter rain' will be given at its close for the ripening of the harvest" (GC 611).

If we would compare the intensity of the former rain with that of the latter rain, we would find out that the second one greatly exceeds the first. Because of the present rate of population growth, the work that has to be done now, humanly speaking, is of an unlimited scope. In order that we may not let an apparently impossible task discourage us, we have divine assurance. "The great work of the gospel is not to close with less manifestation of the power of God than marked its opening" (GC 611). "The outpouring of the Holy Spirit on the day of Pentecost was the former rain, but the latter rain will be more abundant" (COL 121).

The Holy Spirit will operate with such power and effectiveness during the latter rain that He will bring conviction to thousands who otherwise would not respond. They will recognize truth and will gladly heed the call.

"The message will be carried not so much by argument as by the deep conviction of the Spirit of God. The arguments have been presented. The seed has been sown, and now it will spring up and bear fruit. The publications distributed by missionary workers have exerted their influence, yet many whose minds were impressed have been prevented from fully comprehending the truth or from yielding obedience. Now the rays of light penetrate everywhere, the truth is seen in its clearness, and the honest children of God sever the bands which have held them. Family connections, church relations, are powerless to stay them now. Truth is more precious than all besides. Notwithstanding the agencies combined against the truth, a large number take their stand upon the Lord's side" (GC 612).

Interestingly, the Holy Spirit will not do the part of the task appointed for the human instrumentalities. Human voices present arguments; human hands distribute publications. But the Spirit will cause the seed to spring up, convicting the individual to decide for Christ despite human ties and social and religious prejudices.

Purpose of the Latter Rain

If, according to Acts 1:8, the baptism of the Holy Spirit in the case of the individual believer has the specific purpose of enabling him to more effectively proclaim the gospel, it will be much more powerful during the time of the latter rain. The Spirit will be showered upon the church at large to ripen the harvest and to enable the people of God to accomplish a task that otherwise would have been totally impossible.

The prophecy of Revelation 18:1-4 unveils before our

eyes the fast way in which, under the operation of the Spirit, the work of God will finish in a flash of glory. "I saw another angel," writes John the Beloved, "come down from heaven, having great power; and the earth was lightened with his glory" (verse 1). Men and women over the whole earth will hear the call: "Come out of her [Babylon], my people, that ye be not partakers of her sins, and that ye receive not of her plagues" (verse 4).

Obstacles and prejudices have prevented a countless number of people up to now from fully accepting the third angel's message. But the Spirit, poured out without measure in the latter rain, will convict with such a force that many will untangle themselves from all such hindrances and embrace the truth, while others will refuse to do so in spite of seeing it clearly.

Those children of God prepared for the latter rain will receive it gladly, and the Spirit will employ them in a powerful way. But those whose experience is only superficial, who have doubts regarding the possibility of accomplishing the gospel task, will lose the joy of partaking in that work. They have not acquired the fitness for heaven.

Aside from the first great purpose of the latter rain, namely, the conclusion of God's work on earth (GC 611), it has a second and important objective. It enables the children of God to go through the time of trouble triumphantly. In the words of Ellen White, it has to "prepare the saints to stand in the period when the seven last plagues shall be poured out" (EW 86; see also 7BC 984).

We should not forget a key factor in the task of spreading the gospel: the role of our publications (7T 140; Ev 693). Magazines, tracts, and books enter places unreachable by other means and influence people who would never attend evangelistic meetings. Also they have another benefit. A person can read and study printed matter without hurry, and as many times as necessary, until he understands its message. Publications may remain now on the shelves gathering dust for a time, but under the latter rain the Spirit of God will move people to look for them and study them, and He will deeply impress their minds as they read.

Willingness of God to Send the Latter Rain

The beautiful promise of Jesus should convince us that God is more than willing to bestow to His children the Holy Spirit: "If ye then, being evil, know how to give good gifts unto your children: how much more shall your heavenly Father give the Holy Spirit to them that ask him?" (Luke 11:13).

Normally we speak about the latter rain as an important event that has to happen in the future, and we imply that we can do nothing to advance the special time in which the Lord will bring it.

"There are some who, instead of wisely improving present opportunities, are idly waiting for some special season of spiritual refreshing by which their ability to enlighten others will be greatly increased. They neglect present duties and privileges and allow their light to burn dim, while they look forward to a time when, without any effort on their part, they will be made the recipients of special blessing, by which they will be transformed and fitted for service" (ChS 255).

Nothing is further from the truth than the assumption that the latter rain belongs to the future. If the church had taken advantage of its opportunities, if the people of God had reached the needed preparation and had actively proclaimed its message, the latter rain would have fallen, and Christ would have come to this world long ago. "It is not because of any restriction on the part of God that the riches of His grace do not flow earthward to men. . . . If all were willing, all would be filled with the Spirit" (AA 50). "The descent of the Holy Spirit upon the church is looked forward to as in the future; but it is the privilege of the church to have it now" (Ev 701).

"We are living in the time of the Holy Spirit's power. It is seeking to diffuse itself through the agency of humanity, thus increasing its influence in the world" (ChS 251).

Why It Has Not Yet Happened

Nearly all of God's promises to man involve certain conditions, not because God is arbitrary or because He wants to make it more difficult to secure the heavenly blessings, but because the fulfillment of those conditions puts our heart and mind into the only situation in which we can avail ourselves of the spiritual benefits we ask for.

Evidently, if we desire to experience a blessing from the bestowal of God's gifts, we have to feel a real need for them and make room in our heart for Christ and His Spirit. But sometimes our life is so full of other things that it leaves no place for the divine presence. And we cannot serve God and the world at the same time. "He that is not with me," said Jesus, "is against me; and he that gathereth not with me scattereth abroad" (Matthew 12:30). If our mind is full with worldly interests, or selfish motives, or ambitions of power—even in God's work—Christ cannot occupy the throne of our life. We cannot expect the Spirit or the blessings of God if impurity, unforgiven and unforsaken sin, pride and self-sufficiency, or bitterness control us.

Speaking about the Holy Spirit, Mrs. White uses such expressions as "It is given *on conditions*. . . . He is ready to supply every soul *according to the capacity to receive*" (DA 672); "The Spirit works upon man's heart, *according to his desire and consent*" (COL 411).

We will devote our whole next chapter to review the important conditions for the reception of the latter rain.

The Early and the Latter Rain in the Personal Experience

The early and the latter rain symbolize the operation of the Holy Spirit through our lives. The prophet Hosea wrote, "Let us know, let us follow on to know Jehovah: his going forth is sure as the morning; and he will come unto us as the rain, as the latter rain that watereth the earth" (Hosea 6:3, ASV). The KJV renders it: ". . . as the latter and former rain."

The verse employs a beautiful metaphor to illustrate the growing Christian experience. First of all, it says, "Let us know, let us follow on to know Jehovah." In other words, our knowledge of the Lord is gradual and forever increasing. Then it declares, "His going forth [the Lord's presence in our life] is sure as the morning." In the same way as the sun rises in the eastern sky until the perfect noontime, so the grace of God and the operation of His Spirit in our life produces a continuous growth. Then comes the symbol of the former and latter rain.

The former rain represents the first stage of the Christian life. The convicting of the Spirit produces repentance, forgiveness, and forsaking of sin. The abiding presence of the Spirit brings the new birth, purifies the soul, and transforms the life. It is a work of a lifetime and of every day.

In order for the Christian to keep on receiving the former rain, he needs to employ the means that heaven puts at his disposal: the study of the Word, a life of prayer, and active witnessing.

As the Spirit works in the experience of the individual former rain, He prepares the Christian to receive the fullness of the Spirit in the latter rain. "We may have had a measure of the Spirit of God, but by prayer and faith we are continually to seek more of the Spirit. It will never do to cease our efforts. If we do not progress, if we do not place ourselves in an attitude to receive both the former and the latter rain, we shall lose our souls, and the responsibility will lie at our own door" (TM 508).

And Mrs. White explains it even further: "Many have in a great measure failed to receive the former rain. They have not obtained all the benefits that God has thus provided for them. . . . The work that God has begun in the human heart in giving His light and knowledge must be continually going forward. Every individual must realize his own necessity. The heart must be *emptied of every defilement* and *cleansed* for the indwelling of the Spirit. It was by the *confession and forsaking of sin*, by earnest *prayer* and *consecration of themselves to God*, that the early disciples prepared for the outpouring of the Holy Spirit on the Day of Pentecost. The same work, only in greater degree, must be done now. . . . There must be no neglect of the grace represented by the former rain. Only those who are living up to the light they have will receive greater light. Unless we are daily advancing in the exemplification of the active Christian virtues, we shall not recognize the manifestations of the Holy Spirit in the latter rain. It may be falling on hearts all around us, but we shall not discern or receive it" (TM 507).

Chapter 10

Conditions for the Latter Rain

Since the Holy Spirit is a blessing that, "claimed by faith, brings all other blessings in its train" (GW 285), and since without the powerful showers of the latter rain we can have absolutely no hope of finishing God's work on earth, we should ask ourselves, "Is there anything we can do to cause the latter rain to fall?"

The answer is a positive yes. In our previous chapter we saw that it is neither lack of willingness on God's part to bestow on us His gift nor because the Lord has established a definite time in the future for the momentous event that the latter rain is not yet a reality in its fullness. Rather, it is because we, individually and corporately as a church, have not fulfilled the needed requisites. Let us review the conditions that we need to meet in order to see the rain of grace descending on God's people.

Evidently the Lord wanted to outpour His Spirit long before now. He wanted to finish His work a long time ago. The writings of Ellen White repeat that fact over and over. Actually in 1892 she wrote that "the loud cry of the third angel has already begun in the revelation of the righteousness of Christ, the sin-pardoning Redeemer. This is the beginning of the light of the angel whose glory shall fill the whole earth" (1SM 363). But alluding to what happened at Minneapolis in 1888, she also commented, "By exciting that opposition [to the message of the righteousness of Christ preached at that conference] Satan succeeded in shutting away from our people, in a great measure, the special power of the Holy Spirit that God longed to impart to them" (1SM 234, 235).

Hunger and Thirst and Insistent Prayer

The first condition we must meet is to feel a need for the Spirit and to plead fervently and insistently for His reception. "Since this is the means by which we are to receive power, why do we not hunger and thirst for the gift of the Spirit?" (AA 50). "Wherever the need of the Holy Spirit is a matter little thought of, there is seen spiritual drought, spiritual darkness, spiritual declension and death" (AA 50).

How can we feel hunger and thirst for the Spirit? We cannot achieve it by forcing ourselves. Some time ago a plane crashed in the high altitudes of the Andes. Several members of the party starved to death. The hunger of the survivors was so intense that they ate the flesh of their dead companions and managed to live until the rescuers found them. That was real hunger.

Can we feel the deep need of the Spirit to the same degree that a starving person craves food? Yes, we can. But it is another miracle that God creates in us only as we have a daily, living contact with Him and with Christ. The Word of God, which is the sword of the Spirit, cuts its way to the heart of our selfish natures. It convinces us of our sins, frailties, and mistakes, creates in us an understanding of our desperate needs, drives us to our knees, takes us to Christ, gives real meaning and deepness to our prayers, and prepares us for the cleansing and changing action of the Holy Spirit.

We may tell ourselves that the Lord will shower upon the church the Holy Spirit when He sees best. But Ellen White warns us that "we are not to trust to the ordinary working of providence. We must pray that God will unseal the fountain of the water of life. . . . Let us, with contrite hearts, pray most earnestly that now, in the time of the latter rain, the showers of grace may fall upon us. At every meeting we attend our prayers should ascend, that at this very time God will impart warmth and moisture to our souls" (TM 508, 509).

"Meetings," she also wrote, "should be held in every

church for solemn prayer and earnest searching of the word to know what is truth. Take the promises of God, and ask God in living faith for the outpouring of His Holy Spirit. When the Holy Spirit is shed upon us, marrow and fatness will be drawn from the word of God. . . . When the churches become living, working churches, the Holy Spirit will be given in answer to their sincere request. Then the truth of God's word will be regarded with new interest, and will be explored as if it were a revelation just from the courts above. . . . The Bible will be regarded as a charter from heaven. Its study will absorb the mind, and its truth will feast the soul. The promises of God now repeated as if the soul had never tasted of His love, will then glow upon the altar of the heart, and fall in burning words from the lips of the messengers of God. They will then plead with souls with an earnestness that cannot be repulsed. Then the windows of heaven will be open for the showers of the latter rain" (RH, February 25, 1890).

The Experience of the Early Rain

The latter rain cannot come without the early rain appearing first. The latter rain will not do much good if the early showers have not fallen. "Many have in a great measure failed to receive the former rain" (TM 507). "We may be sure that when the Holy Spirit is poured out those who did not receive and appreciate the early rain will not see or understand the value of the latter rain" (TM 399).

The majority of individual Christians should have responded completely and without reservation to the convicting power of the Holy Spirit so that He becomes in their life an indwelling, cleansing power. The Spirit creates in us a Christlike character. Only then will the Spirit through us draw sinners to Christ, as at Pentecost. Unless the ministers and the major portion of the people of God experience a personal Pentecost, there will be no latter rain.

And what is the early rain to which Ellen White refers in the individual experience? She answers, "The heart must be emptied of every defilement and cleansed for the indwelling of the Spirit" (TM 507).

If we want to partake of the latter rain, we cannot procrastinate until some time in the future. Right now, every day of our life, we need to seek the Lord. Every day we must confess our sins, seek forgiveness, and obtain the power of God to forsake them. Surrendering daily, we must live in close contact with God, obeying the voice of the Spirit and acquiring in our life the love of God that can come only from Him.

Obedience: to Be Willingly Guided and Used by the Spirit

A third requisite to receive or to keep the fullness of the Spirit is submission, obedience, willingness to let Him guide and use us. "We are his witnesses of these things; and so is also the Holy Ghost, *whom God hath given to them that obey him*" (Acts 5:32).

Obedience to the voice of the Spirit means to carry out all His orders or promptings. If we resist the instruction the Spirit gives us through the Word of God, and sometimes directly to our heart, we not only lose His abiding presence but also become unfitted to receive the latter rain.

"There are many who believe and profess to claim the Lord's promise; they talk about Christ and about the Holy Spirit, yet receive no benefit. They do not surrender the soul to be guided and controlled by the divine agencies. We cannot use the Holy Spirit. The Spirit is to use us. . . . Many will not submit to this. They want to manage themselves. This is why they do not receive the heavenly gift" (DA 672).

"Today you are to have your vessel purified that it may be ready for the heavenly dew, ready for the showers of the latter rain; for the latter rain will come, and the blessing of God will fill every soul that is purified from every defilement. It is our work today to yield our souls to Christ, that we may be fitted for the time of refreshing from the presence of the Lord—fitted for the baptism of the Holy Spirit" (1SM 191).

Witnessing

God could have chosen to evangelize the whole earth by some extraordinary method or by the direct action of angels. But He decided to give us the honor of associating with Him so that while working on behalf of others we would strengthen our own experience.

We have more and more tended to rely on some organization, program, or method, be it radio, television, or sophisticated public evangelism. But nothing can substitute for personal effort. No organization can replace individual witnessing and person-to-person relationships. The Lord will not pour out His Spirit on machinery, institutions, or organizations. Instead, He will send it to men and women fitted to receive and use it. "The Spirit is poured out upon all who will yield to its promptings, and, casting off all man's machinery, his binding rules and cautious methods, they will declare the truth with the might of the Spirit's power. Multitudes will receive the faith and join the armies of the Lord" (Ev 700).

According to Acts 1:8 Christ promised the Spirit for a specific reason, namely, to witness. But the Spirit will not manifest Himself at His fullest until our people know by experience what it means to witness for God. "This will not be while the largest portion of the church are not laborers together with God" (ChS 253).

Will the Lord have to liberate the church from many of the lukewarm Christians who are not ready to obey the Spirit in proclaiming the gospel of Jesus? "The work is soon to close. The members of the church militant who have proved faithful will become the church triumphant" (Ev 707).

Victory Over Self

When we examine what happened at Pentecost, we discover another requisite needed to make the second Pentecost a reality today. The inspired record reads, "And when the day of Pentecost was fully come, they were *all with one accord* in one place" (Acts 2:1).

"The disciples prayed with intense earnestness for a fitness to meet men and in their daily intercourse to speak words that would lead sinners to Christ. Putting away all differences, all desire for the supremacy, they came close together in Christian fellowship. They drew nearer and nearer to God. . . . These days of preparation were days of deep heart searching. The disciples felt their spiritual need and cried to the Lord for the holy unction that was to fit them for the work of soul saving. They did not ask for a blessing for themselves merely. They were weighted with the burden of the salvation of souls. They realized that the gospel was to be carried to the world, and they claimed the power that Christ had promised" (AA 37).

"When one is fully emptied of self, when every false god is cast out of the soul, the vacuum is filled by the inflowing of the Spirit of Christ" (GW 287). In the case of those who would be blessed by the latter rain, "self-idolatry, which lies at the foundation of all sin, has been crucified" (GW 114). Only under this condition can the Spirit fill us. Pride and self-sufficiency Mrs. White lists as the most hopeless, the most incurable, sin.

In order to protect Paul against this dangerous spiritual ailment, the Lord had to refuse the apostle's request for better health and keep him with "a thorn in the flesh" as a "messenger of Satan," lest he should exalt himself and completely lose the power of the Spirit that accompanied all his labors (see 2 Corinthians 12:7-9).

Up until a few days before Pentecost the disciples continued to argue about who would be the greatest in the temporal kingdom of Jesus. But when they understood the principle that underlies the real kingdom of God—humility, crucifixion of self, meekness, and absolute dependence on Christ—everything changed. Their struggle for supremacy vanished. All bitterness disappeared. With their self-sufficiency and conceit gone, the Spirit of the Master pervaded their hearts. They were all with one accord and ready for the heavenly rain of the Spirit.

Peter also had to learn the same lesson. The hard way. And twice. The first time occurred when the disciples struggled against the storm-tossed waves of the Sea of Galilee. Suddenly Peter recognized the Lord walking on the rough sea. At Jesus' request, Peter began walking from the boat triumphantly toward Jesus. But after a moment, full of joy and pride, he turned from Jesus to glance back to his companions, as if to say, "Look what I am doing!" Immediately he began to sink. When he cried to Jesus in his despair, Jesus took him by the hand and saved his life. "Walking side by side, Peter's hand in that of his Master, they stepped into the boat together. But Peter was now subdued and silent. He had no reason to boast over his fellows, for through unbelief and self-exaltation he had very nearly lost his life" (DA 381, 382).

The second time Peter had to learn the lesson took place at the judgment of Christ. A few hours before, he had claimed that although all the rest might forsake the Saviour, he would remain faithful till the end. How could he have made such a shameful denial? But after Pentecost, totally converted, humble and completely dependent on God, full of the Holy Spirit, he risked his life by refusing to submit to the highest authorities in the nation.

"When we bring our hearts into unity with Christ, and our lives into harmony with His work, the Spirit that fell on the disciples on the day of Pentecost will fall on us" (RH, June 30, 1903).

When we subdue self and no longer contend for titles, power, honor, or position; when we uncover and conquer sin; when love, joy, and peace fill our hearts; when self has died and Christ is supreme in our heart; when our main interest is to finish the God-given task—regardless of our profession or our rank—then we are ready to receive the baptism of the Spirit. And that experience, repeated daily, will take us from the early rain to the latter rain and will prepare the church for the wonderful promise of God's power in the second Pentecost.

Chapter 11

The Finishing of God's Work

While it is completely impossible for human beings to finish God's work on earth without the mighty intervention of the Holy Spirit in the latter rain, it is also absolutely true that God depends on us as His children to do the human part of the task, not because He needs us, but because He wants to confer on us the high honor of serving as His co-workers in the most noble and exciting enterprise on earth.

But God made us His associates for another important reason. Wanting to develop in us a character suitable for eternity, He saw involving us in the proclamation of the gospel as an effective way of helping us to acquire that character. Through witnessing we fully identify with the Master and elevate our Christian experience to heights otherwise impossible for us to reach.

This is why "every true disciple is born into the kingdom of God as a missionary. No sooner does he come to know the Saviour than he desires to make others acquainted with Him. The saving and sanctifying truth cannot be shut up in his heart. He who drinks of the living water becomes a fountain of life. The receiver becomes a giver. The grace of Christ in the soul is like a spring in the desert, welling up to refresh all, and making those who are ready to perish eager to drink of the water of life." Mrs. White concludes, "In doing this work a greater blessing is received than if we work merely to benefit ourselves. It is in working to spread the good news of salvation that we are brought near to the Saviour" (MH 102, 103).

Promises of a Finished Work

God planned that His people Israel would enter the promised land soon after they left Egypt. But because of their unfaithfulness, lack of faith, and murmuring, a journey that normally would have taken eleven days stretched to forty years, with the tragic outcome that the generation that left Egypt had to die in the desert. But finally the Lord managed to fulfill His purpose of having His people take possession of Canaan.

The modern people of God would have long ago reached the heavenly Canaan if it were not for their lack of preparation, their unfaithfulness, and their consequent inactivity. But in spite of it, the Lord will end the misery and suffering of this desert, Planet Earth, and lead His loyal ones into His heavenly kingdom.

John's vision of three angels flying swiftly to proclaim the gospel is a marvelous promise and a prophecy that God will finish the work. The words of Jesus recorded in Matthew 24:14 and many other Bible passages reinforce our certainty that God will triumph.

"When divine power is combined with human effort, the work will spread like fire in the stubble. God will employ agencies whose origin man will be unable to discern; angels will do a work which men might have had the blessing of accomplishing, had they not neglected to answer the claims of God" (1SM 118). But, Mrs. White warns, "This work can be accomplished only by *the whole church* acting their part under the guidance and in the power of Christ" (8T 47; italics in the original).

Aside from the clear prophecies of the Bible predicting the completion of the gospel proclamation—like the one recorded in Revelation 10:5-7—Mrs. White gave us the assurance of a finished task. "Through most wonderful workings of divine providence," she wrote, "mountains of difficulty will be removed and cast into the sea. The message that means so much to the dwellers upon the earth will be heard and understood. Men will know what is truth. Onward and still onward the work will advance until the whole earth shall have been warned, and then shall the end come" (PK 223, 224).

A Special Time for a Clear Message

Never have we seen more confusion in the religious field than now. So many different churches call themselves Christian, yet deny the fundamentals of the gospel. People all over the world are eagerly looking for truth. Thousands of people wander from one church to another in search of the right way. Amid all the confusion, God commands His church to rise to its great opportunity and proclaim with courage, "Babylon the great is fallen. . . . Come out of her, my people, that ye be not partakers of her sins, and that ye receive not of her plagues" (Revelation 18:2-4). The Lord asks His church to shine at the very hour when "darkness shall cover the earth, and gross darkness the people" (Isaiah 60:2).

Ellen White has pointed to a special time when the announcement of the fall of Babylon has to be given with a special emphasis and a special clarity. Up to now, in our publications, in our preaching, we have tried to be cautious, and that has been the right approach in the past.

But when the time comes we will present the mistakes and corruptions of Babylon clearly. "The sins of Babylon will be laid open. The fearful results of enforcing the observances of the church by civil authority, the inroads of spiritualism, the stealthy but rapid progress of the papal power—all will be unmasked. By these solemn warnings the people will be stirred. Thousands upon thousands will listen who have never heard words like these" (GC 606; read, if possible, the whole chapter "The Final Warning").

And although, as in the time of the Protestant Reformation, it will bring persecution, persecution itself will put the church of God and its truth in the spotlight. Newspapers throughout the whole world will feature the confrontation between truth and error, and newscasters on radio and television programs will speak about it, until the issue stirs the whole earth and the arguments for the gospel will stand out sharply in every country.

A Fast and Miraculous Work

The promises and assurances are many that the work of God has to reach a triumphant climax. In 1892 Mrs. White wrote that "the work is soon to close. The members of the church militant who have proved faithful will become the church triumphant" (Ev 707).

"Servants of God, with their faces lighted up and shining with holy consecration, will hasten from place to place to proclaim the message from heaven. By thousands of voices, all over the earth, the warning will be given. Miracles will be wrought, the sick will be healed, and signs and wonders will follow the believers. Satan also works with lying wonders, even bringing down fire from heaven in the sight of men (Revelation 13:13). Thus the inhabitants of the earth will be brought to take their stand" (GC 612).

We should move forward with courage, faith, and a renewed zeal and enthusiasm, using all the wonderful means God has put at our disposal.

The Latter Rain and the Finishing of God's Work

No Biblical passage better describes in symbolic and prophetic form the descent and the work of the Holy Spirit in the latter rain than Revelation 18:1-4. Although God has used and will use literal angels directly in the proclamation of the gospel, the angel of Revelation 18, in the same way as the three of Revelation 14, is symbolic. The word *angelos* in Greek means literally "messenger," although it also designates celestial beings. In this sense John employs the symbol of the heavenly messengers to describe the work that God's people, the appointed human messengers, will do to present the gospel to their fellowmen.

Specifically speaking, the fourth angel of Revelation 18 does not represent a new message or a new group of human emissaries, but it depicts an additional power added to the gospel in its special setting of history's last hour. Actually what the prophet describes here is the latter rain. And the expression "the earth was lightened with his glory" conveys the idea of rapid spread of truth and the convicting power of the Spirit. It will free every sincere person from all ties that bind him to family, church, state, or society. Multitudes, defying ridicule, hardships, persecution, and the threat of death, will accept the seal of God instead of the mark of the beast.

Men and women in high positions will accept the final gospel message. People with great social influence will decide to align themselves with those of God and will bravely defend them, thwarting the efforts of the enemy.

God's power will descend, bringing a renewed spirit of consecration and activity, so that the church will perform an apparently impossible task in an astonishingly short time. But it must reach two main conditions before the mighty power of His Spirit descends.

First Necessary Condition: Sanctification

The Lord cannot conclude His work on behalf of the unwarned people of the earth without first finishing it in our own hearts. "The One who started the good work in you will bring it to completion by the day of Christ Jesus" (Philippians 1:6, NEB). We discovered in an earlier chapter that God cannot even send us the latter rain without a special preparation that the church does not have today.

One of the most meaningful and striking messages Ellen White wrote was that "Christ is waiting with longing desire for the manifestation of Himself in His church. When the character of Christ shall be perfectly reproduced in His people, then He will come to claim them as His own" (COL 69).

Probably the absence of consecration, the lack of sanctification, the failure to have the character of Christ reproduced in our individual lives, is the main reason why we have not yet witnessed the shower of the Holy Spirit. And probably that is why in some countries and in some divisions of the world the work has gone forward much faster and with a much greater display of the power of the Spirit than in other areas. God waits to see His character reproduced in the lives of His people. When that happens, He can fulfill His promise of power and miracle in completing our earthly task. Until then He can act only to the extent of our consecration and activity.

When the ancient people of God, on the eve of their taking possession of the Promised Land, prepared to cross the Jordan, Joshua told them, "Sanctify yourselves: for to morrow the Lord will do wonders among you" (Joshua 3:5).

First the sanctification, then the wonders of God.

Can God visit us with the power of His Spirit when revival and reformation have not yet taken place on a broad basis? Can God bless us with the fulfillment of His promises when extended lukewarmness, worldliness, unfaithfulness, and lack of repentance still exist among us? Can He send us the latter rain when we still have impurity, selfishness, covetousness, pride, contention, strife for supremacy, disunity? Such questions every one of us has to answer personally, because the state of the church is the sum total of the condition of every individual. And the sad thing is that those not willing to let Christ cleanse them from every idol He will at last have to separate from His chosen people. They will forfeit their opportunity of participating in the great triumph of the church and will also lose their eternal life.

Second Necessary Condition: Witnessing Activity

Should we not have any other scripture explaining the individual responsibility of every believer to witness for Christ, the Gospel Commission of the Lord recorded in Mark 16:15 would be enough: "Go ye into all the world, and preach the gospel to every creature." Although Jesus spoke specifically to His disciples, He meant to include every child of God.

In Mark 13:34 the Master illustrated our individual duty and privilege with the following parable: "The Son of man is as a man taking a far journey, who left his house, and gave authority to his servants, and *to every man his work*, and commanded the porter to watch." Not only did he assign every man *his* work, but he spoke to the porter. Normally we consider the porter as a man discharging the smallest responsibility. But the master commanded even him to be on the alert. "The work of God in this earth *can never be finished*," Mrs. White stated, "until the men and women comprising our church membership rally to the work, and unite their efforts with those of ministers and church officers" (ChS 68). Elsewhere she said, "Not more surely is the place prepared for us in the heavenly mansions than is the *special place designated on earth* where we are to work for God" (COL 327).

Each one of us has a specific niche on earth where he can exert his maximum influence, more than any other fellow member, more than any minister. Explaining what happened with the Samaritan woman, Ellen White wrote that "the Samaritan woman who talked with Jesus at Jacob's well had no sooner found the Saviour than she brought others to Him. *She proved herself a more effective missionary than His own disciples.* . . . Through the woman whom they despised a whole cityful were brought to hear Jesus. She carried the light at once to her countrymen" (MH 102). *No one else could have convinced so many Samaritans to come* at the same time to listen to the Saviour. Every one of us has his particular field for which he or she bears responsibility, and where no other one would have so great influence.

"None of us can do without the blessing of God, but God can do His work without the aid of man if He so choose. But He has given to every man his work" (5T 736).

"Let the gospel message ring through our churches, summoning them to universal action. Let the members of the church have increased faith, gaining zeal from their unseen, heavenly allies, from a knowledge of their exhaustless resources, from the greatness of the enterprise in which they are engaged, and from the power of their Leader. Those who place themselves under God's control, to be led and guided by Him, will catch the steady tread of the events ordained by Him to take place. Inspired with the Spirit of Him who gave His life for the life of the world, they will no longer stand still in impotency, pointing to what they cannot do. Putting on the armor of heaven, they will go forth to the warfare, willing to do and dare for God, knowing that His omnipotence will supply their need" (7T 14).

Let us rally to the task. Since "the spirit of Christ in the heart is like a spring in the desert, flowing to refresh all and making those who are ready to perish, eager to drink of the water of life" (SC 77), let us use this wonderful spring of life to save others, and also to prepare our own selves for heaven.

We achieve physical fitness through exercise. So it happens in the spiritual realm. "The Christian who will not exercise his God-given powers not only fails to grow up into Christ, but he loses the strength that he already had" (SC 81). "Strength comes by exercise; activity is the very condition of life." "Those who thus exercise the Christian graces will grow and will become strong to work for God. . . . Those who thus devote themselves to unselfish effort for the good of others are most surely *working out their own salvation*" (SC 80).

Perhaps we should add one more thought here—the therapeutic and healthful effect of carrying to others the gospel. Jesus invited us, "Come unto me, all ye that labour and are heavy laden, and I will give you rest. Take my yoke upon you" (Matthew 11:28). Here the Saviour equates spiritual rest with His yoke, which is work on behalf of others. Nothing relieves worry and anxiety so much as assuming the yoke of Christ, because he who does, comes in close contact with His Best Friend. The yoke is an instrument for two. On the other side of the yoke stands Christ Himself.

"For the disheartened there is a sure remedy—faith, prayer, work. Faith and activity will impart assurance and satisfaction that will increase day by day" (PK 164).

Chapter 12

How to Be Prepared for the Crisis, Part 1

We notice a striking parallel between what happened with Enoch and what God plans to do with His people today. The short statement of Genesis 5:24, "And Enoch walked with God: and he was not; for God took him," summarizes the patriarch's story. The New Testament adds a few strokes to the picture: "By faith Enoch was translated that he should not see death; and was not found, because God had translated him: for before his translation he had this testimony, that he pleased God" (Hebrews 11:5).

As God took Enoch alive to heaven before the Flood destroyed the wicked world of his day, at His second coming Jesus will translate the living righteous to heaven before fire wipes out the earth.

We belong to a unique generation. A mighty display of God's power will deliver those of His people still alive after having passed through the dramatic events of the last hour. God will transform them instantaneously and take them to heaven with Him and His holy angels.

But before then the redeemed need to participate in the same spiritual condition that characterized Enoch's life. In that sense, his life symbolizes the last generation of God's people. Ellen White wrote, "The godly character of this prophet [Enoch] represents the state of holiness which must be attained by those who shall be 'redeemed from the earth' . . . at the time of Christ's second advent" (PP 88, 89).

And she explains further in the same book what his walk with God involved. "Enoch's walk with God was not in a trance or a vision, but in all the duties of his daily life.

He did not become a hermit, shutting himself entirely from the world; for he had a work to do for God in the world. In the family and in his intercourse with men, as a husband and father, a friend, a citizen, he was the steadfast, unwavering servant of the Lord" (PP 85).

In many senses the experience of Enoch was similar to ours. Enriching even more the sketchy, but eloquent, picture of his life presented in the Bible, Ellen White tells us, "Enoch was a man of strong and highly cultivated mind and extensive knowledge; he was honored with special revelations from God; yet being in constant communion with heaven, with a sense of the divine greatness and perfection ever before him, he was one of the humblest of men. The closer the connection with God, the deeper was the sense of his own weakness and imperfection.

"Distressed by the increasing wickedness of the ungodly, . . . [Enoch] spent much time in solitude, giving himself to meditation and prayer. . . . To him prayer was as the breath of the soul; he lived in the very atmosphere of heaven" (PP 85).

Being a man of strong and highly cultivated mind and of extensive knowledge, Enoch possessed a background equivalent to that of the well-educated of our generation. Honored by special revelations from God, his situation parallels that of the Seventh-day Adventist Church, so highly favored by revelations and admonitions from God through Ellen G. White. Distressed by the increasing wickedness of the men of his time, he lived in an age similar to ours. God had revealed to him that a flood would destroy the world, just as He has instructed us that fire will annihilate it.

At the same time Enoch lived an upright life as a neighbor, as a citizen, as a father, as a member of his community. He sensed his special need of help from God to be a living testimony before his fellowmen, and he spent much time and effort on his devotional life. In spite of his godly life, he had a deep sense of his weakness and imperfection.

And God translated him.

How can we achieve in our individual life the same

holiness that characterized his, a state that will enable God to place us among the 144,000, to seal us, and to take us home with Him without seeing death?

Although in the previous chapters we have mentioned several factors that will enable us to attain the special condition we need to belong to God's chosen before Christ's return, we will turn our attention specifically to them in the next two chapters.

Time With God

The disciples had worked hard fulfilling Christ's commitment. But now, after their return from their missionary journey, He invited them to retire to a quiet place with Him. They needed to enjoy not only a little rest but also a period of close communion with the Saviour. "And he said unto them, Come ye yourselves apart into a desert place, and rest a while" (Mark 6:31). In the close and private setting with the future apostles, Jesus could communicate freely with them, correct their mistakes, encourage them, strengthen them for the great task they were soon to do.

As did the disciples, we too require the refreshing company of the source of all power, comfort, and wisdom. Every child of God vitally needs precious moments of private communion with Him. Amid the hurries and worries of life, even in the work of God, every Christian must have time dedicated to his private devotions.

The Master's loving reproach to the busy and concerned Martha also illustrates this point. "Martha, Martha, thou art careful and troubled about many things: but one thing is needful: and Mary hath chosen that good part, which shall not be taken away from her" (Luke 10:41, 42). Every one of us needs "that good part, which shall not be taken away"—to sit quietly at the feet of Jesus, like Mary, and commune with Him.

But the *time* factor is extremely important.

As Enoch spent hours alone with God, we need to devote enough time with Him. We live in an age of hurry. Many voices require our attention. And we try to do everything briefly. Our meetings, our presentations, our articles, our interviews, are short.

But one thing still takes time, even in our day. To develop a love relationship we must invest time. The young man who falls in love with a girl wants to spend as much time as possible with her. As he courts her, he does not count time by the watch. Neither does she. And the more time they take to be together, to communicate with each other, the more they know each other, the more they appreciate each other, the more intense their love becomes.

"It would be well for us to spend a thoughtful hour each day in contemplation of the life of Christ," E. G. White wrote. "We should take it point by point, and let the imagination grasp each scene, especially the closing ones. As we thus dwell upon His great sacrifice for us, our confidence in Him will be more constant, our love will be quickened, and we shall be more deeply imbued with His spirit. If we would be saved at last, we must learn the lesson of penitence and humiliation at the foot of the cross" (DA 83).

May God give us the willingness to cut out the superfluous and secondary things of life in order to dedicate more time to daily communion with God. Only then will we have the strength to win life's battles and, fully prepared, enter with our Saviour in the mansions above.

Alone With God

It had been a busy, tiring day. Hour after hour, an interminable row of sick and needy people in search of comfort and healing had come to the humble home where Christ stayed. And everyone had gone back relieved and whole. Never before had the city of Capernaum experienced such a wonderful day.

Finally, late at night, after Jesus had helped so many, He went to bed. But He did not sleep long hours. While the darkness of the night still enveloped the city, the Master, "rising up a great while before day, . . . went out, and departed into a solitary place, and there prayed" (Mark 1:35).

He knew that another new day, with all its challenges, responsibilities, temptations, and opportunities lay ahead, and in His human dependence upon His Father, He used the quiet hour before dawn to be alone with God. In His experience, that was the hour of power. And it should be also ours.

Family worship is a necessity, a basic factor for a happy home. Worship at church or in groups is also a great source of spiritual strength, indispensable for our Christian growth. But besides those opportunities, our private hour of devotion *alone with God* is an absolutely vital need. Every Christian must meditate alone and talk with his Father alone.

It was during his hour of seclusion with God when Jacob won his great victory, when his character received the needed divine touch and he consequently received his new name. Saul really changed the whole aim and direction of his life during three days he spent by himself with God after his encounter with Jesus on the Damascus road. Without sight, he had enough time to meditate on the scriptures that referred to the first advent of Christ. And there he yielded completely to the Spirit's voice.

During his hour of solitude with God Elijah heard the "still small voice" of the Holy Spirit speaking to his heart and bringing him courage and hope. The Spirit can communicate with us much better when everything is quiet.

The scope of our dialogue with God in family or group worship and in church meetings must be limited in content and in time. But when we are alone with our Father in private devotion, we do not have to worry about time. If we feel that we need half an hour, God will listen to us attentively. And if we spend the whole night meditating and praying about our spiritual problems or pleading for somebody else, He still keeps company with us.

Neither do we need to worry about the subject. Problems that we would not discuss with our best friend or with our spouse, we may feel completely free to open our heart about them with Jesus.

Are we not satisfied with our Christian experience? Do we still feel a vacuum in our life? Do we really long for a more exalted walk with God? Do we need to have more power, a greater measure of the Spirit? We can find the answer at the feet of Jesus, alone with God.

Every Day With God

In diabetes the patient must take insulin by pill or by

shot every day, in addition to following a specific diet and receiving other proper care. Medical science cannot yet heal the disease, but the person can live a normal healthy life every day if he does not miss the insulin. The day he does not get it, his condition suddenly begins to deteriorate, and it keeps on worsening if he continues without the medicine. Death may result.

Likewise, each one of us has acquired from Adam the incurable disease of sin, and we have to wrestle every day with our sinful nature. Inherited or acquired weaknesses or defects of character—actually, inherited sinfulness—threaten every day and make it absolutely necessary to daily receive an appropriate dosage of the power of God in order to live that day a life free from the disease of sin. The Christian life is a permanent war and an upward race without truce or recess.

Romans 7 describes the desperate struggle of man—not only before conversion but also after it. While we are still in sinful flesh—until the coming of the Lord—we will continue to need a constant renewal of our submission to God and a reinforcement of our relationship with Christ. The experience of Romans 8:1-3—describing the man who, by faith in and surrender to Christ, has been made free from the law of sin not only by forgiveness but also by victory—does not do away completely with our war against sin, against self, and against Satan described in Romans 7:7-24.

Naturally, we know that the only way of converting the drama of human failure and desperation of Romans 7 into the glorious victory of Romans 8 is a covenant of faith by which we deliver our will into the hands of the Invincible Conqueror, Jesus Himself. He waits to take over the rulership of our life, fighting our battles, earning victory for us. But we must reenact our covenant of faith and surrender every morning while the Spirit of God speaks to us in the study of His Word and in private prayer.

Paul wrote, "I die daily" (1 Corinthians 15:31). Every day we need to avail ourselves of the imputed righteousness of Christ and to receive a fresh provision of the presence and the power of God. Daily we must renew our personal contact with Heaven.

If we are not constant and regular in our devotional life, we are not safe. "Day by day God instructs His children. . . . It is the issue of the daily test that determines their victory or defeat in life's great crisis. . . . Only through realizing our own weakness and looking steadfastly unto Jesus can we walk securely" (DA 382).

How can we achieve an experience of sinlessness? Scripture answers, "Whosoever abideth in him sinneth not" (1 John 3:6). "So long as we are united to Him by faith, sin has no more dominion over us. God reaches for the hand of faith in us to direct it to lay fast hold upon the divinity of Christ, that we may attain to perfection of character" (DA 123).

To Know Christ Through the Word

People packed the main public auditorium, anxiously awaiting the time for the lecture to begin. They filled every classroom and every inch of space in the hallways of the School of Philosophy and Letters at Buenos Aires University. The school had conveniently installed a public-address system. Never in its history had that institution of learning seen such a huge crowd of eager educated men and women. What happened? Who was going to speak? None other than the famous author and philosopher Ortega y Gasset, who had just arrived from Spain.

How many had met the speaker before? Actually only a few of them had ever seen him. But all those present knew him quite well, and for that reason they had come from all corners of the huge capital city and from the surrounding areas. But how did they know him if they had never seen him? They had read and analyzed his books, and they were familiar with the great thinker's theories and ideas. Admiring the man, they responded to his personality, and his philosophy strongly influenced them.

In order for the Christian to have a vital experience he must really know Christ—know Him as his personal Saviour, as the Master Teacher, as his Greatest Friend, as the Lord of his life, and as the sole source of spiritual power. In that personal knowledge of Christ resides the very secret of eternal life: "This is life eternal," Christ said, "that they might know thee the only true God, and Jesus Christ, whom thou hast sent" (John 17:3).

A practical and experiential knowledge of Christ is so fundamental that Paul wrote, "I count all things but loss for the *excellency of the knowledge of Christ Jesus* my Lord." A few lines later he expressed his longing for that knowledge: "That I may know him" (Philippians 3:8, 10). He had come to know Jesus so well that he really fell in love with Him, conveying his experience in the immortal words, "For me to live is Christ" (Philippians 1:21).

Have we reached this stage in our spiritual development? Is Christ the center of our lives? Can we say conscientiously, "For me to live is Christ"? Or is it something or somebody else?

But the main question is, How do we achieve this complete and wonderful knowledge of Christ that comes with its saving power?

First, by reading and meditating His Word. That audience in Buenos Aires knew the lecturer, though few had really seen him. But they "saw" him in his books. Likewise we "see" Jesus and come to know Him in His Word: "Sanctify them through thy truth: thy word is truth" (John 17:17). So powerful is the Word of God that the psalmist had discovered in it the secret of a victorious life, and he prayed, "Thy word have I hid in mine heart, that I might not sin against thee" (Psalm 119:11). And Jesus referred to the same principle when He admonished His disciples, "Abide in me: . . . for without me ye can do nothing." Immediately He indicated the way of abiding in Him: "If ye abide in me, and *my words abide in you . . .* " (John 15:7).

The Word has power because it is identified with Christ Himself. Jesus is in His Word. Christ is the Word made flesh, and the Word is Jesus made written language. As we eat daily to keep our strength, we need to feed daily on the Word of God, our Heavenly Bread.

A Two-way Communication System

In March, 1947, we traveled from Argentina to study at the seminary, then in Washington, D.C., and to become acquainted with our institutions. The Second World War had just finished. Air travel, not yet popular, was rather expensive, and the passenger liners were not yet reestablished on a regular schedule. So we had to take an American cargo boat with room for a few passengers. We made friends with the officer in charge of the radio system.

"I remember reading that the tragedy of the *Titanic* happened at midnight," I mentioned to him one day, "and the nearest ship that could have come to the rescue did not receive the SOS. At that time the ship radioman had just left his post and gone to sleep. What would happen today if something similar occurred?"

"Come along with me," he answered. "I will show you our equipment. If an SOS message came at midnight, when nobody is on duty, a highly sensitive instrument would sound an alarm. It would ring in the pilot's house and also in my private stateroom. So, you see, there is no way to miss a call like this."

When a Christian needs to get in touch with God, whether because of an emergency or during regular daily devotions, we have the absolute assurance that the call will get through to our heavenly Father. Probably many times God wants to communicate with us, and the message does not go through because our heart is not in tune with Him.

We need to commune with God through prayer as naturally as a child talks with his father. To grow in our Christian experience, we also need to hear Him speaking to us through His Word. Every moment of every day we need to depend on the Holy Spirit.

No matter how high our position, how many years we have been with the Lord, or what our title or status, we need daily private prayer and study. We must refill our heart with the oil of the Spirit, recharge our souls with the Heavenly Power, and receive God's strength for each new day. We cannot have victorious living unless we have daily prayer, study of God's Word, and private devotion.

Our old nature lurks in the shadows, ready to jump out at any moment of carelessness. It constantly strives to revive. Daily, hourly, we need to reaffirm our surrender to Christ and our dependence on Him.

The secret of Christ's greatness and His victory was

prayer. Had He not prayed as He did, He wouldn't have lived as He did. "Prayer in secret, prayer while the hands are engaged in labor, prayer while walking by the way, prayer in the night season, the heart's desires ever ascending to God—this is our only safety. . . .

"We must look to Christ; we must resist as He resisted; we must pray as He prayed; we must agonize as He agonized, if we would conquer as He conquered" (EGW, RH, November 8, 1887).

Study of the Word and prayer are two indispensable tools for victory because they put us in close contact with Christ. And Christ is the only source of a triumphant life. The same kind of continual contact we find between the branch and the vine (John 15:4-7) should exist between ourselves and Christ.

The magic formula for spiritual success is: "Christ in you, the hope of glory" (Colossians 1:27). As we fix our eyes on Jesus, the Author and the Finisher of our faith, and as we behold His beauty, His perfection, His love, we become like Him and reflect His image. May we learn how to identify ourselves completely with the One who is our only hope of victory by devoting time to be alone with God.

Chapter 13

How to Be Prepared for the Crisis, Part 2

The main difference between the wise and the foolish virgins was their preparation for the great event they awaited. Both groups believed that the bridegroom would come soon. And also both went to sleep for a time. But the wise girls had ample provision of oil for their lamps, while the foolish ones had neglected getting extra.

As we know, the oil symbolizes the Holy Spirit, which brings all other blessings in its train. The superficial experience of the unprepared children of God, represented by the unwise virgins, will result in the tragedy of not entering to partake of the marriage feast when the Bridegroom arrives. Their lack of interest in their Christian experience costs them their salvation. Satisfied with going through the externals of religion, they never achieved an intimate and close relationship with Jesus. Mere formalities, mental knowledge without the experience, will prove worthless.

In our previous chapter we began considering the needed preparation to successfully meet the great day of the Lord. We saw that our devotional life is absolutely essential. Only through prayer and study can we make ourselves ready to be clothed with the robe of Christ's righteousness and achieve sanctification.

In this chapter we want to consider other spiritual elements.

Complete Surrender

Some time ago we had the privilege of visiting one of the most beautiful and prosperous countries of Europe—Switzerland. Though geographically small, the nation is politically great and highly respected. One of Switzerland's most outstanding characteristics is that throughout our century it has never gotten involved in any military conflict, and it kept its neutrality during the two world wars.

Likewise, in many issues we can keep our neutrality and refrain from taking sides. But not so in our Christian life. Jesus tells us, "He that is not with me is against me: and he that gathereth not with me scattereth" (Luke 11:23).

At every point of our life we are either under the dominion of Christ or of the devil. There is no neutral position. If we do not make our utmost effort to surrender to Jesus and make Him our Lord, Satan automatically dominates and uses us.

Immediately after the statement of Christ recorded in Luke 11:23, we find the story told by Jesus of the unclean spirit. Once it has gone out of a man, it comes back one day and finds his old house empty. Then it brings another seven spirits more wicked than he and again takes possession of that heart.

Ellen White explains the close relationship between the story and the preceding verse that speaks about the impossibility of being neutral. "There were many in Christ's day, as there are today," she said, "over whom the control of Satan for the time seemed broken; through the grace of God they were set free from the evil spirits. . . . But like the stony-ground hearers of the parable, they did not *abide* in His love. They did not surrender themselves to God *daily*, that Christ might dwell in the heart." So "they were wholly dominated by the power of evil" (DA 323, 324).

Of course man does not need to be physically demon-possessed for Satan to control him. Selfishness, anger, self-sufficiency, envy, hatred, are all manifestations of satanic rulership.

"Unless we do yield ourselves to the control of Christ, we shall be dominated by the wicked one. We must inevitably be under the control of the one or the other of the two great powers that are contending for the supremacy of the world." And then comes an especially impressive and thought-provoking statement: "It is not necessary for us deliberately to choose the service of the kingdom of darkness in order to come under its dominion. We have only to neglect to ally ourselves with the kingdom of light" (DA 324).

We could say that the master key of salvation is the surrender of our will.

A transatlantic freighter arrives at the mouth of the Rio de la Plata, its captain willingly surrenders his command to another specialized captain. The Rio de la Plata is a wide but shallow and treacherous river that separates Argentina from Uruguay. Large ships cannot navigate it except in restricted channels. The ship's captain gladly puts the helm in the hands of the local pilot, who knows that river like the palm of his hand.

In the same way, Jesus is the Captain of our salvation. Having traveled the same road before us, He is perfectly acquainted with every problem and difficulty. Therefore He can lead our life safely and successfully.

But suppose the captain of the freighter rejects the services of the pilot. "I don't need you," he argues. "I have gone through almost all the seas of the world." He would soon discover that he is in deep trouble.

What does it mean to surrender? It simply involves using the will, the master key of our life, to deny ourselves and to choose Christ. God, in His own image, has made man a free moral entity, endowing him with freedom of choice. The Lord never forces our will. He will never save us against our wishes. Instead He says, "I stand at the door, and knock: if any man hear my voice, and open the door, I will come in to him, and will sup with him, and he with me" (Revelation 3:20).

He also says, "Choose life" (Deuteronomy 30:19). To the one who wants to be saved He urges, "Let him deny himself" (Matthew 16:24) and decide to turn to Jesus.

"Many are inquiring," Ellen White wrote, " '*How* am I to make the surrender of myself to God?' . . . What you need to understand is the true force of the will. This is the governing power in the nature of man, the power of decision, or of choice. Everything depends on the right action of the will. . . . You cannot change your heart, you cannot of yourself give to God its affections; but you can *choose* to serve Him" (SC 47, italics in original).

As the case of the ship requires a change of command, so also in our life there should be a shift of rulership. "I am crucified" (Galatians 2:20), explained the apostle. Self has died. The throne of the heart stands vacant. Self has been denied. And then Paul adds, "Christ liveth in me." Once self has surrendered completely, Christ takes over and occupies the throne.

When He comes into our heart, Christ brings His love, His joy, His peace, His patience, His long-suffering, His gentleness, His goodness, His faith, His meekness, and His self-control. Our life changes completely. It is a peaceful life, a godly life, a victorious life.

But, we insist, it is not enough to make the choice once. We need to renew it every moment. It should become in us a way of life. Because, "as long as Satan reigns we shall have self to subdue, besetments to overcome, and there is no stopping place" (7BC 947).

"Through the right exercise of the will, an entire change may be made in the life. By yielding up the will to Christ, we ally ourselves with divine power. We receive strength from above to hold us steadfast. A pure and noble life, a life of victory over appetite and lust, is possible to everyone who will unite his weak, wavering human will to the omnipotent, unwavering will of God" (MH 176).

Cleansing From Sin

The first result of yielding to the voice of the Holy Spirit and of not resisting the "goodness of God," which "leadeth . . . to repentence" (Romans 2:4), is forgiveness and cleansing from sin. The tender words of Jesus spoken to the palsied man, "Son, be of good cheer; thy sins be forgiven thee" (Matthew 9:2), "fell like music on the sufferer's ear" (DA 268) and are the same ones that Christ directs to every repentant person.

The children of God will never, on this earth, reach the point where they may dispense with the forgiving grace of the Saviour and the imputed righteousness of Christ. No matter how much we grow in our Christian life, no matter how many victories we win in the name and power of God, regardless of how far we go in sanctification, we always keep a sinful nature. So we will continue to depend on the perfect life of obedience of our Heavenly Substitute and His atoning death in our behalf. We will always require repentance and forgiveness of sin, will always need acceptance of God through the merits of Christ.

Actually, the nearer we are to God, the closer we walk with Jesus, the better we understand His holiness and the more intensely we feel our shortcomings and deficiencies. More and more we realize our need to lean on the infused righteousness of the One who is our only righteousness. Repentance, let us say it again, is not an isolated act that belongs only to the beginner, but it is an experience that should be ever present in our life. It causes us to feel more keenly our defects and trespasses the nearer we approach our Saviour, until the day when God "shall change our vile body, that it may be fashioned like unto his glorious body" (Philippians 3:21).

After stating that "if we say that we have no sin, we deceive ourselves, and the truth is not in us [that is the typical assertion of the Laodicean]," John declared, "If we confess our sins, he is faithful and just to forgive us our sins, and to cleanse us from all unrighteousness" (1 John 1:8, 9). And a little bit earlier he had said, "The blood of Jesus Christ his Son cleanseth us from all sin" (verse 7).

We should notice that with forgiveness and peace also comes absolute cleansing from sin. The Lord not only *pronounces* us perfectly clean because He offers His blood as our substitute in a work of atonement, but His healing power actually *makes* us clean from sin. He infuses in us a hate for sin when we see that our sin has made it necessary for Christ to die on our behalf. As Jesus not only forgave the palsied man and made him happy but added the spiritual healing and cleansing of which the physical healing was just a symbol, the Saviour does the same with every contrite heart.

Total Victory

Genuine repentance should yield results. "Confession will not be acceptable to God without sincere repentance and reformation. There must be decided changes in the life;

everything offensive to God must be put away. This will be the result of genuine sorrow for sin" (SC 39). Forsaking sin and gaining victory over our sinful tendencies, both the inherited and the ones that we acquired from our environment, are unavoidable corollaries of our repentance.

But the child of God has an always-present and treacherous enemy: self. It is woven into the threads of our personality and character. Ellen White wrote under divine inspiration, "Each one will have a close struggle to overcome sin in his own heart. This is at times a very painful and discouraging work. . . . Everyone who enters the pearly gates of the city of God will enter there as a conqueror, and his greatest conquest will have been the conquest of self" (9T 182, 183).

What is this "self"? It is simply our carnal nature, our own heart before God performs the heavenly operation of taking "the stony heart" out of our flesh—a heart hardened by sin, selfishness, jealousy, worldliness, hatred, strife for supremacy. Then He gives us a "heart of flesh" (Ezekiel 11:19), tenderized by the work of the Holy Spirit and the love of God. Self is our pride, our self-sufficiency, our self-esteem; self is our bitterness, our anger, our revenging spirit, our lack of a forgiving disposition. In other words, self is our lack of Christ.

Such traits are so imbedded in our characters that they constitute an integral part of our personality. We do not have to cultivate such feelings and thoughts. They naturally belong to the lower nature that governs us. The law of sin ties our hands (Romans 7:23). But praise the Lord, our victory is assured, since Paul added, "The law of the Spirit of life in Christ Jesus hath made me free from the law of sin and death" (Romans 8:2).

Even after a person is born again, the law of sin—self, if you please—still lingers, and it will do so until our glorification. The struggle will continue until the end. True, God cleanses us from our defilement, and the Holy Spirit creates in us pure thoughts, lofty ideals, love for our fellowmen. But this comes only as a result of our direct contact with Christ, the sole source of power, holiness, and purity. On the other hand, we are able to maintain such an experience only while we keep that union with Jesus. "Abide in me," He says. "Without me ye can do nothing" (John 15:4, 5).

The real struggle is not against our sinfulness or character defects. It is subduing self to Christ, letting Him take over. The battle we must wage is to surrender completely to Him and to remain in His wonderful keeping.

Faith

Along with surrender we need faith.

Many people have worried for years about how they can overcome weaknesses, character defects, and specific sins. Obviously God's plan for our lives includes not only forgiveness but also victory. And if He plans something for us, He provides the means.

In the Word of God we find that, along with the surrender of self, the road to victory over sin is faith. Commenting on the paralyzed man at Bethesda, Ellen G. White wrote, "Through the same faith we may receive spiritual healing. By sin we have been severed from the life of God. Our souls are palsied. Of ourselves we are no more capable of living a holy life than was the impotent man capable of walking.

"There are many who realize their helplessness, and who long for that spiritual life which will bring them into harmony with God; they are vainly striving to obtain it. In despair they cry, 'O wretched man that I am! who shall deliver me from this body of death?' (Romans 7:24, margin). Let these desponding, struggling ones look up. The Saviour is bending over the purchase of His blood, saying with inexpressible tenderness and pity, 'Wilt thou be made whole?' He bids you arise in health and peace. Do not wait to feel that you are made whole. Believe His word, and it will be fulfilled. Put your will on the side of Christ. Will to serve Him, and in acting upon His word you will receive strength" (DA 203).

Somebody may say, "Yes, but I have an inherited weakness. I was born with a damaged nervous system, and I cannot control my temper." Others may exclaim, "I have let my thoughts wander so much that it is impossible for me to refrain from impure thinking."

Ellen White assures us that "whatever may be the evil

practice, the master passion which through long indulgence binds both soul and body, Christ is able and longs to deliver. He will impart life to the soul that is 'dead in trespasses' (Ephesians 2:1). He will set free the captive that is held by weakness and misfortune and the chains of sin" (DA 203).

Along with prayer, surrender, and watchfulness, faith is the road to victory. "This is the victory that overcometh the world, even our faith" (1 John 5:4). It is a miracle that we cannot explain. The gospel of Jesus Christ stands above psychology, and no science can contain the mystery of godliness within its limits.

If up to now we have failed to conquer some of our spiritual weaknesses, let us seize the arm of God by faith, accept Him at His word, and after committing our feebleness to Him, act as if we were whole, since by His grace and by His power we are. "So long as we are united to Him by faith, sin has no more dominion over us. God reaches for the hand of faith in us to direct it to lay fast hold upon the divinity of Christ, that we may attain to perfection of character" (DA 123).

"Through faith in Christ, every deficiency of character may be supplied, every defilement cleansed, every fault corrected, every excellence developed. 'Ye are complete in Him' " (Ed 257).

"Unto him that is able to keep you from falling, and to present you faultless before the presence of his glory with exceeding joy . . . be glory and majesty" (Jude 24).

"We have no power to free ourselves from Satan's control," Mrs. White wrote, "but when we desire to be set free from sin, and in our great need cry out for a power out of and above ourselves, the powers of the soul are imbued with the divine energy of the Holy Spirit, and they obey the dictates of the will in fulfilling the will of God. The only condition upon which the freedom of man is possible is that of becoming one with Christ" (DA 466).

Obedience, "Fruits Meet for Repentance"

When John the Baptist preached his powerful message of repentance, he said to his audience, "Bring forth therefore fruits meet for repentance" (Matthew 3:8). Profession without a practical demonstration is of no value. Obedience must necessarily follow repentance and surrender.

Many modern revivals that make a high profession of following Jesus but without any reform in the practical life are not genuine. "Let no man present the idea that man has little or nothing to do in the great work of overcoming; for God does nothing for man without his cooperation. . . . From first to last man is to be a laborer together with God" (1SM 381).

So obedience will be the natural result of a real surrender to the will of God and a true desire to change. "Wrongs cannot be righted, nor can reformations in conduct be made by a few feeble, intermittent efforts. Character building is the work, not of a day, nor of a year, but of a lifetime. The struggle for conquest over self, for holiness and heaven, is a lifelong struggle. Without continual effort and constant activity, there can be no advancement in the divine life, no attainment of the victor's crown.

"The strongest evidence of man's fall from a higher state is the fact that it costs so much to return. The way of return can be gained only by hard fighting, inch by inch, hour by hour. In one moment, by a hasty, unguarded act, we may place ourselves in the power of evil; but it requires more than a moment to break the fetters and attain to a holier life. The purpose may be formed, the work begun; but its accomplishment will require toil, time, perseverance, patience, and sacrifice.

"We cannot allow ourselves to act from impulse. We cannot be off guard for a moment. Beset with temptations without number, we must resist firmly or be conquered. Should we come to the close of life with our work undone, it would be an eternal loss.

"The life of the apostle Paul was a constant conflict with self. He said, 'I die daily' (1 Corinthians 15:31). His will and his desires every day conflicted with duty and the will of God. Instead of following inclination, he did God's will, however crucifying to his nature. . . .

"The Christian life is a battle and a march. In this warfare there is no release; the effort must be continuous and persevering. It is by unceasing endeavor that we maintain the victory over the temptations of Satan. Christian integrity must be sought with resistless energy and maintained with a resolute fixedness of purpose.

"No one will be borne upward without stern, persevering effort in his own behalf. All must engage in this warfare for themselves; no one else can fight our battles" (MH 452, 453).

Diligent Witnessing

Since we are dealing here with how to make sure of our readiness for the great final crisis and for translation, we will mention only the spiritual benefits of the personal witnessing that God expects from us. First of all, we should remember that when Christ has really filled our heart, we will feel a drive, a need to share with others what He has done for us.

"All who receive the gospel message into the heart will long to proclaim it. The heaven-born love of Christ must find expression. Those who have put on Christ will relate their experience. . . . It is unnatural for any to keep these things secret, and those who are filled with the love of Christ will not do so. In proportion as the Lord has made them the depositaries of sacred truth will be their desire that others shall receive the same blessing." And notice now the tremendous benefits they will obtain: "And as they make known the rich treasures of God's grace, more and still more of the grace of Christ will be imparted to them. They will have the heart of a little child in its simplicity and unreserved obedience. Their souls will pant after holiness, and more and more of the treasures of truth and grace will be revealed to them to be given to the world" (COL 125).

Commenting on the feeding of the five thousand, Ellen White wrote, "We can receive only as we impart to others. As we continue imparting, we continue to receive; and the more we impart, the more we shall receive" (DA 370).

When Christ invited the heavily burdened to come to Him to find rest, He directly related that rest with His yoke: "Come unto me, all ye that labour and are heavy laden, and

I will give you rest. Take my yoke upon you" (Matthew 11:28, 29). Normally we prescribe inactivity to the exhausted and overburdened. But Christ invites them to take His yoke, which represents work and fulfillment of Christian duties. Although it may seem a paradox, the fact is that the person who experiences more spiritual rest and happiness is the one who, responding to the call of the love of Christ, proclaims more earnestly that love to others.

Witnessing is an indispensable part of a victorious experience, of a life ready to meet the Lord. When the apostle Paul described the different parts of the armor that the Christian needs to win his battle against evil forces, he said that our feet should be "shod with the preparation of the gospel of peace" (Ephesians 6:15). In other words, the proclamation of the gospel is a necessary part of our Christian experience.

God reserves for the last generation of His children the most exciting experience of history. We will witness the latter rain in its fullness, and as a result, the conclusion of the last message to the world. But before that, God wants to finish the transformation of our hearts so that we may be completely ready for the crisis prior to His coming.

He has given us a full armor in order for us to be real winners, members of the church triumphant. It is up to us to make use of this protective covering so that we can go successfully through the impending conflict, meet the crisis with victory in the name of Jesus, and rejoice in the glorious consummation of the work of God. Only in that way can we meet our Lord in peace and enter eternity with Him.